You Are a Prize to Be Won! demonstrates the incredible power of story. As I read Wendy's narrative of the airport scene with her boyfriend, my eyes were suddenly opened and I thought to myself, "Oh, my word, that's *me!*" When I am reading a book and I see myself over and over on the pages, I know God is using that book to speak to me. There is so much healing in revelation and this book provides just that revelation. The plain truth is—I'm not the same after reading Wendy's book!

Stacy Hord
Speaker and Author, *A New Vision for Dating*

Opened up Wendy Griffith's manuscript to do the "polite" scan of the pages so I could come up with a proper, "polite" endorsement . . . and ten chapters in I can't pry myself away from it! Engaging, real, authentic and deeply personal . . . this book challenges me, inspires me and makes me feel a little bit braver in my own journey as I walk with Wendy on hers. There have been a million little "me too!" moments that I've stumbled across as I read . . . and any woman, single or not, who has ever struggled to move past "the ex" or to "let go and let God" will be able to relate. What a refreshing and moving look at the journey of the modern, single Christian woman!

Mandy Hale
Creator of *The Single Woman* blog; Author, *The Single Woman: Life, Love & a Dash of Sass*

I stand in awe of Wendy's honesty, wit and painfully learned truths in *You Are a Prize to Be Won!* It's a heartfelt clarion call for women to realize that they are worth much more than a second thought text message or an "I love you, but . . ." It's a roadmap that will help women to love themselves well, and shows why others should too!

Charlene Israel
Anchor and Reporter, CBN News

Wendy Griffith is an intelligent, accomplished, beautiful woman. To simply look at her, one would assume that she lives a charmed life without care or pain. Looks can be deceiving. In this book, Wendy opens her heart and her life to help us realize that we are valued beyond our imagining and loved with an everlasting love. It is in our deepest loss and our greatest pain that we discover the "Lover of our Souls"—the One who is always true, never leaves and knows our deepest longings. Read Wendy's book! Be encouraged, embrace healing and open your heart to a new beginning. You *are* a prize to be won!

Terry Meeuwsen
Co-host, *The 700 Club*; Founder, Orphan's Promise

YOU ARE A PRIZE TO BE WON!

YOU ARE A PRIZE TO BE WON!

don't settle for less than God's best

WENDY GRIFFITH

Revell

a division of Baker Publishing Group
Grand Rapids, Michigan

Published by Revell
a division of Baker Publishing Group
PO Box 6287, Grand Rapids, MI 49516-6287
www.revellbooks.com

Revell edition published 2017
ISBN 978-0-8007-2521-1

Previously published by Regal Books

Printed in the United States of America

Library of Congress Control Number: 2017936725

Back cover photo by Gus Evangelista.

Some names and places have been changed to protect privacy.

To my future husband:
I know you will be worth the wait!

CONTENTS

ACKNOWLEDGMENTS

The person who blesses others will prosper;
he who satisfies others will be satisfied himself.
PROVERBS 11:25, CJB

When you go through heartbreak, you don't go through it alone. There are so many people I want to thank for being there for me.

But first, I want to thank my heavenly Father and Jesus Christ my Lord and Savior for helping me through the hardest year of my life. Lord, You were with me every step of the way, and You're the One who told me to write about my "test." You called it a test and told me that if I obeyed You, I would be rewarded. I know that this book is one of those rewards. I love You and will worship You forever.

Second, I want to thank the girls in the CBN Newsroom: Charlene Israel, Andrea Garrett, Heather Sells, Julia Williams, Lorie Johnson, Donna Russell and Faye O'Neal. Ladies, thank you for listening, praying, crying and laughing with me. I couldn't have survived without you—especially you, Charlene. You were a rock to me on so many days. Thank you for being there, my precious sister and friend.

Special thanks to my CBN hairdressers Alexis Bailey and Christy Montoya. It's really true that our hairdressers know everything about us. And these two ladies know everything! They helped keep my hair looking good even as I shed many tears under the blow-dryer. I love you both dearly and pray that God will repay you for your endless love and counsel—and for all the great hair days!

My makeup artist at CBN knows almost as much as my hairdresser, but I have to keep my mouth closed more during makeup sessions. Many thanks to Sheila Roddy, Pam Sams and Tanya Gasser who cheered me on and never complained when they had to fix my makeup because of tear streaks down my face. Your tender love and care during this challenging time in my life was deeply felt and appreciated. I love you all.

CBN wardrobe stylist Sherry Wade and Judy Roberts from the scheduling department, thanks for all the mama hugs and the great advice. And Judy, thanks for the best chocolate-chip cookies in the world—they saved me many a day.

Special thanks to my real-life sisters JeanAnne Roberts and Nancy St. John. Thanks for being my best friends as well as wonderful sisters. Your phone calls, pep talks and prayers helped me more than you'll ever know. I love you forever.

Deepest thanks to my friend Libby Starks. God sent you into my life at just the right time. Your emails, letters and prayers have been a source of life, comfort and hope to me. I know we'll be friends forever. Many thanks to my dear friend Marguerite Evans, whose wise counsel and deep spirituality helped me understand my pain and regain my focus. Also, many thanks to the countless prayers prayed by my friend and intercessor Susan Watkins; your wisdom and humor and deep spirituality helped me more than you'll ever know. Big rewards are waiting for you in heaven! Hanisha Besant, many thanks for your love and prayers and great Indian tea. What a blessing you were exactly when I needed you. I'm so thankful for our friendship. Reverend DorotheLée Withers, what can I say? It's been a wild ride, and you were with me—thanks, DorotheLée, for being such a great sister, friend and prayer warrior! I also want to thank my friends and intercessors Diane and Cathy. What a blessing to have you in my corner for such a time as this!

And very special thanks to my youngest brother, Truman Griffith, a great dad, husband and attorney in Charleston, West Virginia. You turned out to be the perfect editor for my book. Truman, thanks for your endless hours of reading the chapters and making them better. Your insight was invaluable, and I was so glad to have a man's perspective on a book for women. I love you dearly. And to my other brother, Pete Griffith, also an attorney and a father, thanks for being a great dad and husband and brother. You and Truman are living proof that there are great guys out there who know how to love their women and their sisters.☺

I love you.

Thanks too to my good friend Minyon for your great editing skills and advice. You showed up at the perfect time!

And last, thanks to everyone else who has somehow walked with me on my journey from heartache to wholeness. I thank you from the bottom of my heart. May the Lord shower you with His love and kindness just as you showered me in my time of need.

PREFACE

He heals the brokenhearted and binds up their wounds.
PSALM 147:3, *NIV*

My heart was crushed—but somehow I was still breathing. It had been just a week since my breakup with a man whom I had once believed was the love of my life when Dr. Pat Robertson, founder and chairman of the Christian Broadcasting Network, called me into his office.

Like a concerned father, Pat gently commanded, "Wendy, come in here. Tell me what happened." The compassion in his voice caused the tears that were already close to the surface to come flooding down my cheeks. I reached for the box of tissues on his desk and told him everything. Robertson, a man who has sat down with presidents and kings, a man who once ran for president of the United States and who formed a global media empire, wanted to hear about my heartbreak. I was deeply moved.

After I had finished talking, Pat gave me some heartfelt advice. "Wendy, you are special. You are beautiful, and you are talented. Don't throw yourself away!"

At the time I wasn't quite sure what Pat meant by, "Don't throw yourself away," but apparently God wanted me to remember it, because Pat said it over and over during our short time together. "*Don't throw yourself away!*" Later I figured it out. He meant, "Don't settle. Don't throw yourself away on a guy who is not worthy of you, because you are worth so much more than you realize."

Ah, but knowing our worth, knowing our true value—that's not always easy. There are many reasons why we as women cannot properly gauge our worth. Whether we've been raised by parents or a parent who simply didn't know how to nurture and raise an emotionally healthy child, whether we have allowed society, men or a man in our past (or present) to define who we are instead of what God says about us, or whether we have endured cheating, physical abuse or emotional abuse at the hands of a man we thought would always protect us, there are numerous reasons why women enter relationships with the wrong men. The bottom line is we begin to believe the lie that we're really not worth that much, and we end up being attracted to men who can never truly love us the way we long and deserve to be loved.

The Bible says, "As [a man or woman] thinketh in his [her] heart, so is he [she]" (Prov. 23:7, *KJV*).

Do you know your incredible value? Do you know what you are truly worth? The way you answer this question—or, more importantly, what you truly believe is the answer to it—has the power to change everything in your life. Everything! The way we perceive ourselves, whether as royalty or peasants, as worthy of love or unworthy, will dictate not only how we treat ourselves but how others treat us. It will influence everything from how much favor we receive at work, to how our boyfriends and husbands treat us, to whether we fulfill our God-given destinies.

Many of us have not seen ourselves as God sees us. The enemy of our souls has painted a bleak picture of who we are (not worthy of love, not talented, not beautiful, too young, too old, too fat, too skinny, not smart enough, etc.), and unfortunately, we have believed the lies and not lived up to our potential.

If you're ready to dive into this book, I promise that you are about to find out what your true value is. The lies of the enemy are about to be demolished in your life, and you are about to come forth as the radiant and mighty woman of God that you were always meant to be.

> You shall also be [so beautiful and prosperous as to be thought of as] a crown of glory and honor in the hand of the Lord, and a royal diadem [exceedingly beautiful] in the hand of your God (Isa. 62:3, *AMP*).

My sister, God has a special word for you that will change your life. You are a royal daughter of the Most High King, a princess in the palace, a pearl of great price and beautiful beyond measure. Your greatest love, the man of your dreams and the father of your children, is out there waiting for you, because you, my sister, are *a prize to be won*!

1

THE TEST

When He has tested me, I shall come forth as gold.
JOB 23:10

As the freezing temperatures kept me inside on that cold January morning, I prayed. Standing in my kitchen, where I often do my morning devotions, one word kept playing loudly over and over in my head: *test . . . test . . . test!*

My immediate reaction was *no . . . no . . . no!* I said, "Holy Spirit, I don't want to be tested." But the word continued playing through my mind: *test . . . test . . . test!* I continued to protest, "Lord, this cannot be good—I don't receive this." But as much as I tried to ignore it, I couldn't escape the voice of the Lord. I finally surrendered. "Okay, Lord, if You want to test me, my heart is Yours."

What happened about 12 hours later would prove to be the test of my life.

FLASHBACK: APPROXIMATELY ONE YEAR EARLIER

It was almost Christmas 2010, but I was already looking ahead to Valentine's Day. I was 40-something, single, never-been married, and after way too many lonely weekends, I was ready for romance. I saw on the Internet that one of my favorite musicians, pianist Jim Brickman, was performing in Virginia Beach a few days after Valentine's Day. Perfect! Only one problem—I needed a date to take to the show.

In an act of complete faith, I went online and bought two tickets to Brickman's "An Evening of Romance" concert slated for February 19, 2011. One ticket for me and one for the man I prayed that God would send into my life by the time the concert rolled around.

God did not disappoint. In late January 2011, I received an email from a guy named Michael. He had seen an interview that I had given about being a single Christian that was featured on a Christian dating website, and he was contacting me in response to that. His email was charming and funny. Michael clearly stood out from the rest of the "interesting" inquiries I had received in response to my no-nonsense interview in which I had urged men to man up and not be afraid to ask women out! We began emailing and talking regularly after his first email.

We immediately recognized how much we had in common. Like me, Michael was in his 40s, had never been married and had a career in media. Most importantly, I felt that he might be the type of strong Christian man that I was looking for. Certainly on paper he appeared to be the perfect guy for me. By late February things were falling beautifully into place, and I had a date to the concert!

As the weekend of the concert neared, I was excited to meet Michael for the first time in person. He drove from his hometown to mine the night before the concert, as we were eager to make this weekend last as long as possible.

We met for dinner at a local restaurant. I arrived before Michael did and positioned myself so that he would see me when he walked in. But despite all our common interests and the great conversations we'd had via email and phone up to that point, when our eyes first met, I didn't feel any sparks. I was disappointed, to say the least. Don't get me wrong—Michael was tall with dark hair and deep brown eyes, definitely handsome—but where was the spark? I almost immediately had that sinking feeling that told me, "Back to the drawing board." But I did my best to put that sentiment aside, desperately hoping I was wrong.

Fortunately, as the weekend progressed, so did my feelings. I really wanted to give this guy a shot. He seemed so perfect on paper, and I didn't want to give up too soon.

As the weekend came to a close, Michael and I decided that we definitely wanted to see each other again. It was a surreal feeling. I hadn't dated anyone with this much potential in a long time, and I wondered, *Could he be "the one"?*

Since Michael lived several hours from me, whenever we saw each other, we did what I like to call marathon dating—he would stay in a hotel, and we would go out Friday night, during the day Saturday, Saturday night, and go to church on Sunday morning. Michael usually didn't leave for home until late Sunday night.

My lonely weekends were no more. I looked forward to the doorbell ringing on Friday evenings, followed by romantic dinners down by the sea and strolls along the beach. I especially loved having someone special to go to church with. After years and years of watching other couples snuggle up in church, I finally had my man.

Although it took me a while to fully warm up to Michael, by mid-summer I was unmistakably in love. Somehow Michael had managed to unlock the door to my heart, when no one else, except for my first love back in college, had ever seemed to be able to find the key.

After about five months of dating, I started doing what girls in love sometimes do—hinting about rings and wedding destinations and such. I was sure that Michael felt the same way I did, and I had already semi-jokingly told him, "I am not on the five-year plan"—especially at my age! So one hot July evening, after a romantic dinner, I flirtatiously asked him, "So do you think I am 'the one'?"

Michael had hinted many times that he thought I was, so I was not expecting his answer: "I don't know," he said with some sadness. I was shocked, to say the least, and a little bit mad.

After the initial shock wore off, I asked angrily, "Why are you kissing me the way you're kissing me, then?"

"Because I'm attracted to you," he said.

I'm attractive but not marriage material? Is that what I had just heard this guy say to me? I felt as if I had just been kicked in the gut. All I knew was that the carefree rug of the last five months had suddenly been yanked out from under me. I was in a free fall. In that moment I realized that I deserved better, but I didn't know exactly what to do about it or how to do it. I was already so emotionally invested in this relationship—wasn't he? How could this guy who drove several hours every weekend to see me, spent big bucks on hotels, dinners and flowers and kissed me passionately, not see me as "the one"? (See chapter 14 about the dangers that come with recreational kissing.)

I needed some answers. Later that night, as we sat on the beach, Michael told me that he had doubts about our relationship because of the way I had treated him when I was on the road for work, reporting in New York and elsewhere around the country during the previous months. "I didn't feel like I had a girlfriend when you were traveling," he told me. "You were so cold and distant."

I apologized. Perhaps he was right. I had been a bit heavily focused on work, but truth be told, that had been months before, when I still hadn't been too sure about us. But now I was head over heels for this guy, and he was telling me he didn't feel the same way.

By the end of the evening and after our talk on the beach, I felt a bit better. Perhaps Michael simply needed to know that I was there for him before he could make a serious commitment. However, sleep did not come easily for me that night, and to make matters even worse, when I finally did fall asleep, I had one of the worst dreams of my life. Michael and I were arguing in the dream, and he shouted, "It's over!" Then I woke up.

As I sat up in my bed, I felt paralyzed with fear. Was the dream from God or from the devil? Was it a "warning" dream or the signal of a done deal? All I knew was that fear had seized every part of my being. As irrational as it may sound, I felt as if the circumstances were all my fault. The enemy of my soul had ruthlessly pushed the "rejection button," and my life would never be the same.

REFLECTIONS

1. We know that we can't please God without faith. Have you ever purchased an item or done something in faith to demonstrate that you believed that God would send the right person? Is this something we should do?
2. Should you ask a guy if he thinks you are "the one," or should you wait until he speaks his mind on the subject?
3. Have you ever had your "rejection button" pushed? How did you handle it?

2

I LOVE YOU BUT . . .

Return to the stronghold, you prisoners of hope.
Even today I declare that I will restore double to you.
ZECHARIAH 9:12

After a brutal end to the month of July, given Michael's revelation that I may not be "the one," August became the month from hell. In my panic to become the perfect girlfriend and to convince Michael that he was wrong about me, I began the hard labor of working to make him fall in love me. The irony was striking. Here was a guy with whom I had felt hardly any sparks when I had first met him, and I had convinced myself to give him a chance—and now I was trying to convince him that I was worthy of his love.

Since one of Michael's complaints was that he hadn't felt as if he'd had a girlfriend when I was traveling and that I had seemed distant, I now tried to always be there for him, encourage him and cater to him. I tried to do what I thought he wanted and needed me to. But his heart had gone cold. I could feel it. Suddenly, after months of feeling so beautiful, desirable and relaxed with Michael, I felt like chopped liver. He seemed remote and detached. I blamed myself for this change. I determined to keep working to make him see how wonderful I really was.

By the end of the month, I was exhausted. I felt that I had done all I could to save the relationship. I called Michael from Atlanta, where I was on assignment, and told him that I needed a break—that I had put my heart on the line and wasn't getting anything in return. He sounded concerned but didn't try to talk me out of it. I told him that there was no excuse for the way he'd been treating me.

For example, two weeks earlier, I had taken Michael to my favorite hiking spot in Virginia, Old Rag Mountain, nestled in the beautiful Shenandoah National Forest. I had been so excited to share this experience that I'd had so many times before, with the man I thought I was in love with. But almost from our first steps up the rugged mountain, Michael hiked in front of me, not with me, almost as if it were a race and not a wonderful time in nature with his girlfriend. I'm in pretty good shape, but I had a hard time keeping up with his long-legged strides. And right before we began our trek, he had thrown his backpack on the ground in frustration because I was "taking too long" to put moleskin on my heels so I wouldn't get a blister. The memory of that, plus the fact that he was nowhere in sight and I ended up hiking alone, had brought me to tears. I had been on that mountain so many times before, and never had I felt this sad or alone, even when I was hiking solo! On our way down I tripped on a root, badly bruising my thigh and leaving a nice long scar on my elbow. I had never fallen while hiking on this mountain before. Maybe God was trying to tell me something.

Before Michael and I hung up the phone, I suggested that we take a break—at least two weeks off. He agreed. I could hardly eat that night, my stomach was so tied in knots. My cameraman, who was with me in Atlanta, prayed with me for God's will and for peace, something I desperately longed for and needed.

But the next morning, as I was on my knees in the hotel, praying that Michael would fight for me, my phone rang. I couldn't believe it—it was Michael's number. God was answering my prayers. I said hello, and it was obvious that Michael was crying on the other end. With his voice still quivering, he said, "I've been crying for 12 hours. I can't imagine not seeing you for two weeks. I'm going to drive to Virginia to see you when you get home tonight."

I was thrilled. It was the old Michael! He had seen the light—or so I thought.

I Don't Know If You're "the One"

Even though it was a short flight, it seemed as if the trip home took forever. I couldn't wait to see my boyfriend. As I walked down the long corridor to the baggage claim, wearing my Virginia T-shirt and my blue jeans, I couldn't believe my eyes! I caught a glimpse of Michael standing in the crowd, his six-foot-three frame towering above the eager people waiting for their loved ones to appear. I hadn't known that he was going to meet me at the airport!

I ran to him, and he took me in his arms and kissed me. It was like a scene right out of the movies, and quite romantic! It was after nine in the evening, but a local Italian restaurant was still open, and Michael took me out for a late dinner. We were in a corner booth, and the waitress had already taken our orders. That's when, over the loud clatter of smashing plates, I thought I heard him say, "I love you . . ."

"I'm sorry," I told him, "could you please repeat what you just said?"

Then he said with disturbing clarity, "I came here to tell you that I love you, *but I don't know if you're 'the one.'*"

It was like being kissed and slapped really hard at the same time. His words were what I had desperately longed to hear except for the "but." Had he only stopped after "I love you," it would have been the perfect end to the perfect evening. But he hadn't. Is there supposed to be a "but" after an "I love you"?

Something felt terribly wrong with what Michael had said. Simply put, he had rejected me again. Only this time, to soften the blow, he had put the words "I love you" in front of the hurtful words. Yet even after this, my fear of rejection kept me from standing up for myself. I naively told myself, *He just needs more time.*

Beautiful September

Boy, was I glad to say good-bye to August and hello to September. September would turn out to be one of Michael's and my most memorable and fun months together. The near breakup we'd almost had in August seemed to have softened Michael's heart. He was now frequently telling me that he loved me. He seemed to enjoy saying it, and I felt that he meant it.

We both celebrated our birthdays in September, so we decided to take a special trip together. Neither one of us had ever been to Bermuda, so we thought going there would be a great adventure and something we could share for the first time together.

Yes, we got separate rooms (we didn't believe in sex before marriage). We even stayed at a Christian resort that had morning prayers and a pastor in residence and the most beautiful private beach. We nicknamed it the love lagoon, although there wasn't any love-making going on, only kissing. I had to keep reminding myself that I was not on my honeymoon. (I don't recommend going away to a gorgeous secluded location with your boyfriend, by the way—wait for your honeymoon.) I actually think Michael and I were on better behavior than normal in Bermuda, because we knew the temptations would be great, and we didn't want to cross a line we would regret, but I am thankful that the Lord kept us from making a mistake even in that little love lagoon.

We celebrated Michael's birthday with a wonderful meal at an ocean-side table. We could hear the waves crashing against the cliffs as a thankfully distant hurricane made itself known. After dinner we were drawn to the sounds of music playing in another section of the resort and ended up slow dancing the night away under the Bermuda stars. We didn't do any fast dancing that night, or any other night, because Michael would never fast dance with me—even if we were in a group of strangers. He said it was too embarrassing and that he felt as if people were watching him. I could never understand that, because I love to dance, but it's one of those little things you compromise on when you're in love—and I was definitely in love during that trip to Bermuda.

To top off a perfect month, when we got home from our island getaway, CBN celebrated 50 years of broadcasting with an unprecedented black-tie event on October 1. Michael wore a perfectly fitted black tuxedo, and I wore a long mermaid-style red dress. He was my Rhett Butler, and I was his Scarlett O'Hara. Oh, if life were only as perfect as the photos we took that night.

Before we knew it, autumn had arrived, and Thanksgiving was only days away. The leaves were changing in the same way I thought and hoped that my life was about to change. I was anchoring the news the day before Thanksgiving, when on the set of the *700 Club* Dr. Pat Robertson asked me, "So Wendy, what are you thankful for this year?"

I wasn't expecting the question, but I answered it without hesitation. I proceeded to glowingly tell Pat and a worldwide audience, "Pat, I'm so thankful that I have a boyfriend this year! It's been a long time." I was genuinely happy and wanted the whole world to share in my joy. The camera cut back to Pat and former *700 Club* co-host Kristi Watts smiling and giggling, sharing in my happiness.

After work, I was still laughing to myself about my on-air exchange with Pat and couldn't wait to call Michael. It had been a great day, and I couldn't have felt better.

Before I had a chance to call him, though, I saw that he had emailed me. I thought Michael would be thrilled that I had mentioned him on international television and that his email would reflect that. When I opened the message, however, I saw that it was hardly enthusiastic. "That makes about the sixth or seventh time you've mentioned me on TV," he wrote with a tone that said, "Stop doing that!" Nothing about my performance or how I had looked during the show—only a harsh one-liner that brought tears to my eyes.

Another fiery dart hit my heart. Yes, I had mentioned Michael a couple times on my daily show, CBN Newswatch, but never on the *700 Club*! I was grieved, and because I was still "working" to make him fall in love me, all I could say when I replied to him was, "I thought you would be a little more excited." When he realized that I was upset, he said something to comfort me, and I forgave him.

This was our pattern. I would come on too strong, in his opinion, then he would back away or do or say something hurtful, then I would get upset or say that we needed a break, and he would come running back. It's known as the cat-and-mouse game, and we were playing it.

I began to feel heartbroken—even though we were still together. Something in me (the Holy Spirit no doubt) was urging me to take a break from the relationship, but Michael and I had already booked plane tickets for a Thanksgiving trip. We planned to visit both of our families during the holiday, since they lived in cities fairly close to each other in nearby states. I felt trapped. Friends told me that the feeling would pass and that everything would work out, and I prayed that they were right. I really wanted Michael to be "the one."

Steelers vs. Bengals

For years my family has celebrated Thanksgiving at my sister Nancy's house in Pittsburgh. She, her husband John, and my niece Sydney are huge Steelers fans. After all—Pittsburgh is the heart of Steeler Nation.

Michael was from Cincinnati and just as devout a Bengals fan, maybe even more devoted to his team than my sister's family was to theirs. He had actually gone so far as to tell me at one point that I had to hate the Steelers! When he said this, I thought he was joking, so I said, "I'm a Christian—I can't hate the Steelers!" Besides that, I'm from West Virginia and had gone to West Virginia University, only about an hour from Pittsburgh. I had grown up rooting for the black and gold. How could I possibly hate the Steelers? But Michael insisted, "No, you have to hate the Steelers!" He even bought me a Bengals T-shirt, which I did wear because I wanted to be a good girlfriend and because I liked the black and orange colors. (But in my heart of hearts, I never hated the Steelers!)

So there we were at my sister's home in Pittsburgh over Thanksgiving, and suddenly my sister and I heard yelling from the television room, where Michael and my brother-in-law John were in front of the big screen. The Bengals weren't even playing, but Michael was so mad that the Steelers were winning that he had become vocal about it. It was an uncomfortable scene for John, who was trying to be a good host.

The next day we went to downtown Pittsburgh ("downtown" is pronounced more like "dun-tun" if you say it with a Pittsburgh accent), and my six-year-old niece wanted to buy a #7 Steelers jersey in honor of quarterback Ben Roethlisberger, her favorite player. Michael was so anti-Steelers that he would not even walk into the Steelers store with us. Instead, he stubbornly stood outside on the cold street corner while we bought our Steelers paraphernalia. Michael, suffice it to say, was in "Steelers hell," and there was no escaping. Much to his relief, we moved on to Bengals country the next day.

I may never understand men's fascination with football, but one thing I do know: The man God has for me will never choose his loyalty to an NFL team over his loyalty to me.

Soon the Christmas season was upon us, and the magic of the holidays seemed to keep our relationship floating along quite nicely. Michael and I picked out our first Christmas tree together—a real one! He strung lights along my deck as I baked homemade cookies, and we gave each other special ornaments. Michael gave me a rugged wooden ornament with the word "faith" engraved on it. I gave him a gorgeous blingy one displaying the words "Our First Christmas." The ornaments were perfect, and I had faith that this would be our first of many Christmases together. Yet even though Michael's actions said that we were headed that way, my heart wasn't convinced that he shared the same faith in our future that I had.

Every Christmas until this one, I had desperately longed to have a boyfriend for whom I could buy gifts. This year I had one, and I was determined to spoil him. I got Michael tons of gifts. Among them were two tickets to the Temptations, his favorite Motown group that would be playing near Virginia Beach in February. But my favorite gift for him—and his favorite gift (it seemed)—was a video I had made for him of our year together. The pictures and music brought tears to our eyes as we watched a year's worth of memories dance before us. It was a priceless moment and worth all the work I had done to put the video together.

I thought we were finally making the turn to something deeper. But my tears of joy would soon turn into tears of sorrow as the New Year approached.

REFLECTIONS

1. Has anyone ever told you, "I love you but . . ."? How did you react?
2. Why should there never be a "but" after the words "I love you?"
3. Why is it so important not to make excuses for a significant other's bad behavior, especially in the beginning of a relationship?

3

TIME TO LET GO

A broken heart is a reminder of our only source of power.
ELISABETH ELLIOT

At the end of an anti-climatic New Year's Eve (okay, I'm being nice—
Michael was a total jerk), I returned to the hotel where I was staying near Michael's house, wondering all the way, *Why is he acting so
strangely?* My sparkly gold dress had seemed to go unnoticed. When
I had changed my mind on the kind of steak I wanted to order, Michael had snapped at me, as if it were a sin for a woman to change
her mind. And my boyfriend's passionless kiss at midnight was the
icing on the cake of a deeply disappointing evening. *It's New Year's
Eve!* I had spent the evening thinking, *We're young! We're in love* (so I
thought), *and we have ridiculous party hats on! Why aren't we having fun?*

Even though the writing was clearly on the wall, I refused to read
it. I had convinced myself that I was in love with Michael and that
our problem was that we simply needed to take our relationship to
the next level.

I think what I longed for more than anything was simply to be
wanted. A marriage proposal would certainly be proof that I was not
only wanted but was worthy of being loved. Looking back, though,

I see that getting engaged would have been like having a boulder tossed to me when I was drowning—it would only have made things worse. A woman has to know her own value and must love and respect herself before she can be part of a healthy love relationship. I refused to admit, however, that I was drowning and that Michael was certainly no life raft.

The next day, New Year's Day 2012, I left the hotel and drove over to Michael's house. Evidently surprised to see me, Michael burst into tears, saying that he thought I had perhaps left town early because he "didn't know what to say last night." How a man cannot know what to say to his girlfriend on New Year's Eve is beyond me. How about, "You look amazing," or, "I'm so happy we've had this year together." Still, Michael's tears convinced me again that he really did love me! (The cat and mouse game again. Hello, Wendy! Is anybody home? Apparently not.)

I began to pray in earnest, *Lord, please let him propose!* My friends were praying, and even my little nieces Madison, Sydney and KellyAnne were praying.

But my heart could not lie. I wrote in my journal on January 7, 2012:

Lord, why does my heart feel so broken? Heal my heart, dear Lord. Do heart surgery on me, Lord. Please reveal what's going on; deliver me from the things that are holding me back. I need Your love, Lord. I need You.

Soon after the first of the year, Michael and I decided again to take a couple weeks off from seeing each other to seek the Lord's direction for our relationship. I was delighted and finally felt that Michael was taking some leadership in our future.

When we got back together in mid-January, he said to me, "We've been seeing each other for almost a year now, and we need to ask God how we can bring our two lives and careers together. God clearly brought us together." I agreed with him. We held hands and prayed. It was beautiful. Michael asked God to show us how and when.

But a few days later, during a time of fasting and prayer for our relationship, I had another disturbing dream, this time that Michael would choose to walk away for good. But I refused to believe it. I also heard in my spirit, *It's time to let go.* I shrugged it off saying, "That can't be God." This revelation certainly did not fit into my plans.

The Test

It was now late January, almost one year to the day since I had received that first charming and entertaining email from Michael. We hadn't seen each other in two weeks, but I would see him that night. As I sat in my kitchen doing my morning devotions, I looked through the blinds at the frost on the grass, hoping and praying that our reunion would be warmer than the icy cold outside. It was then that I heard those fateful words in my spirit: *test . . . test . . . test!*

The words were so loud—almost deafening in my mind. I told the Lord that I didn't want to be tested, that I wasn't prepared for a test. But the words continued in my head: *test . . . test . . . test.* That's when I finally gave in and said out loud, "Okay, Lord, if You want to test me, my heart is Yours."

That evening when we got together, Michael was visibly uneasy. Sitting on my red leather couch, I asked him what was wrong and if the Lord had spoken to him. He became quiet and then burst into tears. He said, "I was watching you on TV, and the Lord said to me, 'The world needs her more than you do. Give her back to Me.'"

It was my turn to burst into tears. I was in shock. This could not be happening, but it was. Michael was crying so hard that all I could do was try to comfort him. Why would the Lord tell him that? I didn't know what to do or say. I didn't mention the dream I'd had or the words I'd heard: *It's time to let go.* This was all so raw and painful. Then I remembered what the Holy Spirit had said to me only 12 hours before as I had stood in my kitchen: *test . . . test . . . test . . . !* This was my test.

Maybe this was a test of our relationship, like when God asked Abraham to sacrifice his beloved Isaac so that God could see if Abraham loved Him more than he loved Isaac.

Now it came to pass after these things that God tested Abraham, and said to him, "Abraham!"
And he said, "Here I am."
Then He said, "Take now your son, your only son Isaac, whom you love, and go to the land of Moriah, and offer him there as a burnt offering on one of the mountains of which I shall tell you (Gen. 22:1-2).

Of course, for Abraham, God had provided a ram in the thicket for the sacrifice, and Isaac's life had been spared once God knew that Abraham would have gone through with it. Would God spare Michael's and my relationship as well?

I didn't know. All I knew was that it felt as if my heart was being ripped out of my chest and all my hopes and dreams for happiness and a loving husband were being shattered in a million and one pieces. I was numb.

JOURNAL ENTRY

Father, how do I live? How do I go on without the love of my life? Father, help me. Remember me, Lord. Look upon Your daughter who waits upon You—who looks only to You, Lord. Father, You long to forgive and leave a blessing instead. Your heart is for me, not against me; You are just but also loving and merciful. Father, we're both asking for a second chance, for a ram in the thicket, Lord. Don't kill it, Lord, resurrect it!

I didn't sleep at all that night.

The next day was Sunday, January 29, 2012—the last day of CBN's January Telethon drive. How was I going to go on the air? Somehow, the Lord, as He always does, gave me His strength. Before the tragic events of the night before, Michael had been planning to come to the studio with me that morning so that we could spend more time together. He asked me, "Do you still want me to come?" Still in shock and not quite believing yet that we were really breaking up, I answered, "Yes, I think it will help me if you are there."

Seconds before I went on, I looked over and saw Michael standing against the studio wall, always taller than everyone else. No one suspected anything because they had seen us together plenty of times and knew that we were dating. This was surreal. I still loved him. How was I going to turn that off? Was there a button somewhere that I could push?

Pete, my floor director, gave me the countdown: "Standby—it's coming to you in three, two . . ." Thank God for Pete. After 10 years of doing Telethon together, words weren't necessary for us to communicate. He simply gave me a look that said, "You got this, kid; you're going to do great."

I gave Pete the two tickets to the Motown Temptations Concert that I had bought for Michael and me as one of his Christmas presents. Since Michael and I wouldn't be going to the concert now, I couldn't think of a better or more deserving person than Pete to give the tickets to.

Funny thing was, even after the breakup Michael had still wanted to go to the concert with me as "friends." "I'll pick you up and take you to the concert and then take you home afterward," he had suggested.

"You mean no kissing, no holding hands?" I asked him.

He thought for a moment, then answered, "Yeah, I'll just drop you off at your door." After a year of seeing each other every weekend as boyfriend and girlfriend, a year of kissing and romance, he'd had the nerve to want to go to the concert as "just friends."

How can some people turn things off so quickly? It made me realize that I was a whole lot more invested in our relationship than he was. Michael even said to me, "Does it really have to be all or nothing?" Here we were, two single people in our 40s, who I thought had been dating with the goal of marriage. "Yes. I am worth *all*!" I said.

I was furious with myself when I realized that I'd gambled my heart on someone who saw me as something he could just take or leave.

Mourn and Move On

Michael continued to email me after this, but I refused to answer his emails as they were all the same, ambiguous and double minded. I wanted a man who knew what he wanted—not someone who wanted to keep me around just in case. About a week after our breakup, having had no contact with Michael, I heard a phrase in my spirit: *Mourn and move on*. I heard it so clearly. The Lord wanted me to mourn the loss of the relationship and move on—although it was easier said than done.

Still, after about a week of constantly crying, not sleeping and barely eating, the anger phase began, which actually brought an incredible amount of clarity to me. I realized that, although I had loved Michael, I had not loved myself and had settled for "emotional crumbs" when the Lord had so much more for me. Of course, I was angry about Michael's rejection of me, but I was also angry at myself. Only God could heal this pain. Thankfully, He had promised to do just that: "Be of good courage, and He shall strengthen your heart, all you who hope in the LORD" (Ps. 31:24).

REFLECTIONS

1. Have you ever heard the Holy Spirit tell you to let go or to break off a relationship with someone? How did you feel about it?
2. The Bible says that there is a time to mourn. Why is mourning the loss of a relationship so important?
3. How long should you mourn? Is it different for everyone and with every relationship?
4. How do you know when your heart is healed and you're ready to date again?

4

MY GUARDIAN ANGEL

When you pass through the waters, I will be with you;
and through the rivers, they shall not overflow you. When you walk through
the fire, you shall not be burned, nor shall the flame scorch you.

ISAIAH 43:2

It was a Saturday morning, two weeks since the official breakup, and I was tempted to sleep in a bit longer, especially on this cold February morning. But weekends were too painful, Michael's absence was too tangible—I needed to stay busy. Plus I had a strong sense that I should get up and go hiking. I tossed and turned, hoping the thought would pass, but it was too late. I felt that if I didn't go, I would be missing something. In fact, I was pretty sure I heard the Holy Spirit say, *"Don't miss it!"*

It's a four-hour drive from Virginia Beach to my favorite hiking spot, Old Rag Mountain—one of the most challenging and spectacular hikes in the Blue Ridge Mountains of the Shenandoah National Park in Northern Virginia.

My friend Bob, who lives closer to the mountain than I do, was also hiking Old Rag that day, so I called him and asked if he would meet me at the summit at sunset so we could walk down the mountain together. By the time I gathered my backpack and hiking boots and then stopped for gas and water, it was eleven. I thought to myself, *Wow, I'm getting a late start. I must be crazy.* But I didn't want to "miss it"—whatever "it" was.

It was a beautiful day, sunny, windy and cold at about 45 degrees. I still had to stop for lunch and for bandages for my heels, but I told myself, *If all goes well, I could start hiking by three and make it to the summit by sunset,* which would be around five thirty. The traffic on I-64 West was steady, and I was making good time, when I glanced over at the car next to me and noticed its vanity plate: "GDNANGEL." Guardian angel! It was a sign.

The last time I had hiked Old Rag by myself, the clouds above me had made the shape of a giant angel. It had been so beautiful and clear, and I never forgot it. I felt the Lord was reminding me that when I go hiking, my guardian angel goes with me. Now He was reminding me of that fact again.

One of the best parts about hiking in the Shenandoah Valley is the drive there. Oh, I just love the rolling green hills dotted with black cows, bales of hay and the occasional rustic red barn. And it's worth slowing down to go through the quaint country towns with their little country stores where people are so friendly and you can still get a Coke in a glass bottle.

I arrived at Old Rag around three and quickly put on my boots, scarf, gloves, hat and backpack, which was filled with water, snacks, cell phone and a windbreaker, and I headed up the steep paved road that leads to the head of the trail. I saw two other hikers looking at a map, but other than that it looked as if I would be enjoying some solitude—just me, the Lord and the mountain. As many times as I've climbed Old Rag, I always marvel at what an awesome playground God made it to be for His children. And being from West Virginia—well, you can take the girl out of the mountains, but you can't take the mountains out of the girl.

Although I often hiked alone, the last time I had been on this mountain was with Michael, and the memory was still painful. He had made me cry on this mountain, and part of the reason I needed to make this hike was to forgive him and then to reclaim this mountain as the gift from God that it was.

The hike up was going well. I needed to make good time if I was to meet my friend Bob around five thirty and enjoy the sunset from Old Rag's summit. I ran into a few people, including an Amish family (the girls wore dresses to hike in), making their way down the mountain. I also saw two beautiful deer. One had a gorgeous white tail, and both deer stopped to stare at me as I gazed back at them, mesmerized by their beauty.

As I approached the famous rock scramble of Old Rag, the wind became really wild. In the more than 10 years that I'd hiked this mountain, I could never remember the wind being so loud or so powerful.

Normally it would have frightened me, but that day on the mountain, in the wind and the cold, I felt God's heart for me. As tears streamed down my face, I felt the Lord whisper in the wind, *Wendy, I know how much this hurts you; it hurts Me too. Don't despair, daughter; your Father who loves you is mighty to save. I will repay, daughter. Don't worry; keep climbing, keep forging ahead. Your Father fights for you, and you will not be ashamed.* I can't explain it, but I felt as if the Lord's heart was breaking along with mine. He really does feel our pain.

I wiped the tears from my cheeks and focused in on the most challenging part of the rock scramble. There is a section that is so difficult to maneuver that I've always needed either a push from behind or a hand up from above to finesse it. But today there was not a soul in sight. I prayed, *Lord, show me a foothold or a handhold that will allow me to propel myself up this rock.* I thought back to my rock-climbing days in which I had to use my head as much as my strength. I'm not exactly sure how I did it, but within a few minutes, I was able to figure out a way to use momentum and to push my body up through the crevice to the other side.

I felt a nice sense of accomplishment, but I had no time to rest. The clock was ticking, and I needed to keep a good pace to make it to the top before dark.

As I got closer to the top, the biting wind became too much for my fleece jacket. The windbreaker I'd packed was a lifesaver, and I shivered at the thought that I'd almost left it behind. I figured that my friend Bob was already waiting for me at the top, since he had gotten an earlier start, and was probably watching my progress from his lofty vantage point. I hoped he was staying warm. Bob is an experienced climber and knows Old Rag like the back of his hand, so I wasn't too worried.

Finally, I arrived at the summit—3,291 feet of pure adventure and adrenaline. Usually I love to linger at the top, having a bite to eat and talking to fellow hikers. But on this late February day, the wind was whipping so hard that I had to steady myself against a rock so I wouldn't be blown away. And it was *cold*!

I looked around for Bob. "Bob!" I yelled. No answer. To my disbelief there was no one at the top—not a soul. I yelled again, "Bob!" No one, not even Bob apparently, was crazy enough to be up there in this weather except me. I took my cell phone out, but the battery was drained, and it was too low for radio use. No way to contact Bob.

My mind immediately went into self-preservation mode. *Okay, I need to make use of every ounce of daylight that's left to get down this mountain.* The hike down usually took about two hours—if I moved pretty fast. I had hiked down Old Rag more times than I could remember, and many times at night—but never alone.

I guessed that I had maybe 20 minutes of daylight left. *Lord, I prayed, keep the lights on as long as possible.* I had a small flashlight, although I did not look forward to needing to use it. So I hightailed it down the mountain.

The trail is steep with a lot of rocks, roots and switchbacks, so I couldn't run, but I went as fast as I could. The race was on, but the darkness was inevitable. The last time I'd been on Old Rag, I had taken a pretty bad spill coming down, so my mantra was, "No close calls, no falls."

I kept thinking about the vanity plate I had seen on the way to the mountain, "GDNANGEL." Yes, God had wanted me to see it. He had wanted to remind me that He was with me. *God sees me right now*, I thought. *He's with me. He knows that I've gotten myself into a potentially dangerous situation—and His angel is with me.*

Psalm 91:9-12 says:

Because you have made the LORD, who is my refuge, even the Most High, your dwelling place, no evil shall befall you, nor shall any plague come near your dwelling; for He shall give His angels charge over you, to keep you in all your ways. In their hands they shall bear you up, lest you dash your foot against a stone.

As the trail widened, I began running. I passed two shelters, Byrds Nest, and then a little later, Old Rag Shelters. Often there were campers or hikers having a bonfire or cooking out in these spots, but I had no such luck that night.

By this time, the moon was out, and darkness had fallen over Old Rag Mountain. *If I can make it to the Fire Road, then it will be just two miles in the pitch black dark until I reach the top parking lot! God, help me!* I wasn't worried at all about bears—I figured they were hibernating—but I wasn't sure what other predators were in these woods: wolves, coyotes, mountain lions maybe? And if they were there, I was sure they were hungry. As long as I was running, I didn't feel too scared. But I'm not a runner, and my legs were not cooperating.

I spoke to every part of my body, "Legs, be strong! Heart, be strong! Lungs, be strong!" My backpack was heavy with my unused water, so I poured two bottles out on the ground, which lightened my load considerably. I could run a bit faster now, but I still had to take breaks to walk.

I heard what I thought were coyotes howling. Thank God my flashlight was working! I kept thinking about the fact that God had allowed me to see that vanity plate. He knew that it would bring me some much needed peace and comfort. I'd have felt better if I could actually have seen the guardian angel—but hadn't Jesus said "Blessed are those who have not seen and yet have believed" (John 20:29)? *Lord, help my unbelief.*

I tried to stay focused on getting down the mountain as fast as possible and not on tomorrow's potential headline: "News Anchor Found Eaten by Wolves." I pushed my body to the limit. My recent trips to the gym and the hiking I'd been doing were paying off.

I finally made it to the Fire Road. The moon was just a sliver, but it was brilliant, and the stars were breathtaking. As scared as I was, I still marveled at the beauty of God's creation. And the good news was, I didn't think much about Michael—I was too busy thinking about staying alive.

I continued to run and walk, run and walk. I passed the one-mile marker. *Only about a mile and a half to go.* "God is with me," I said out loud. "He is my defender." I sang as I ran, "Your love is amazing, steady and unchanging, your love is *a mountain, firm beneath my feet!*" I knew that nothing could happen to me apart from God's will and I had many promises of protection from the Word of God:

> The LORD is my light and my salvation—whom shall I fear? The LORD is the stronghold of my life—of whom shall I be afraid? . . . For in the day of trouble he will keep me safe in his dwelling; he will hide me in the shelter of his sacred tent and set me high upon a rock (Ps. 27:1,5, *NIV*).

> You are my hiding place; you will protect me from trouble and surround me with songs of deliverance (32:7, *NIV*).

> The angel of the LORD encamps around those who fear him, and he delivers them. Taste and see that the LORD is good; blessed is the man who takes refuge in him (34:7-8).

> I lift up my eyes to the hills—where does my help come from? My help comes from the LORD, the Maker of heaven and earth.

He will not let your foot slip—he who watches over you will
not slumber; indeed, he who watches over Israel will neither
slumber nor sleep. The LORD watches over you—the LORD is
your shade at your right hand; the sun will not harm you by
day, nor the moon by night. The LORD will keep you from all
harm—he will watch over your life; the LORD will watch over
your coming and going both now and forevermore (121:1-8).

A bit into my second mile on the Fire Road, as I spoke to my
legs, "Be strong!" I saw something move ahead of me—something big
and black. Actually, it looked like several things moving. I zoomed
in with my flashlight.

What I saw brought me huge relief: a group of hikers coming
down the mountain without any flashlights. Thank God! Humans!
I had never been so happy to see people than I was at that moment.
As I approached them, one of the guys in the group said to me, "Wow,
you're brave, coming down the mountain in the dark by yourself."

"It wasn't by choice," I stated honestly.

This guy was a Marine who had recently returned from Afghanistan. To be called brave by a Marine felt pretty cool. He and I com-
pared the night sky of Afghanistan to the incredible starry display
above us. "It's even more beautiful in Afghanistan," the Marine told
me. "The stars seem so much closer and brighter because there isn't
any other light competing for their attention."

The rest of the hike was all downhill and pure joy. I told the
group about missing my friend Bob at the top, and they described
him to a T. "Yeah, we saw him up there," they said. It turns out
that Bob had gotten a little restless waiting for me and had gone
back down the mountain to see if I was stuck at that tricky part.
He used the faster "escape route" to backtrack instead of the main
trail. Otherwise he and I would have run into each other.

But suffice it to say, there would have been no real story if Bob
had shown up. Not only did God speak to me profoundly in the
wind, comforting my heart and sharing in my pain, but He showed

me that He can take care of His children in our most difficult, scary and even dangerous situations. He simply wants us to trust Him.

God knows that I love adventure, and perhaps my scary hike down the mountain was just what I needed in the aftermath of my breakup with Michael. Actually, it was exactly what I needed. I needed to feel alive. And even though I had a hard time walking the next day, I'm sure glad I didn't "miss it"!

Thanks, heavenly Father. Walking with You is always an adventure.

REFLECTIONS

1. Have you ever felt that God was speaking to your heart through nature?
2. Have you ever had an experience in which you were terrified but had never felt so alive?
3. Why is it so important during the healing process to forgive those who have hurt us?
4. What can you learn when you go through a scary or a challenging experience?

5

"YOU GOTTA BELIZE IT!"

Have I not commanded you? Be strong and of good courage;
do not be afraid, nor dismayed, for the Lord your God
is with you wherever you go.
JOSHUA 1:9

Trying to concentrate on work was useless. I needed to escape.
I wanted a quick fix for my hemorrhaging heartache. I needed to
get away—far away.

I had recently met a lady online who had asked me to write some
articles for her Christian women's website. We barely knew each other, but Cathy lived right on the ocean in Belize and had a heart for
hurting women—and I was a hurting woman. I emailed her and told
her my situation. She didn't hesitate. "Come on down," she told me.
"We'll go snorkeling and biking, and it'll help you take your mind
off things."

On February 29, 2011, I left cold and dreary Virginia Beach (well,
it may have been sunny, but everything seemed dreary to me during
those days) and boarded a plane for Belize. This would be my first
trip to Central America. After landing in Belize City, I boarded a

small "puddle jumper" for the final flight. It was packed with excited tourists, most who were on their way to go scuba diving.

Belize is known as one of the world's greatest scuba diving and snorkeling destinations because of its breathtaking underwater scenes. The view from my small window on the plane was spectacular as well: miles and miles of turquoise ocean dotted with little brown islands, much of it seemingly untouched by humanity.

Normally I would have felt a lot of excitement. I have always loved to travel and explore new and exotic locations, tasting the local cuisine and shopping for souvenirs. But today I was merely happy to be away from every reminder of Michael—although my grieving heart, which was still mysteriously beating within my chest, was a constant reminder that I couldn't run away from the pain. Oh, but I was praying for a quick fix.

I landed at the small airport in San Pedro and was greeted by a very tan, short, barefooted and blonde woman named Cathy. I liked her right away. I knew that she and Belize were going to be exactly what the doctor had ordered. There's a great saying in Belize—"You gotta Belize it!"—and I was trying hard to "belize" that I could recover quickly from the worst heartbreak of my life.

My first day there we were up early. I would much rather have stayed under the covers that morning, but Cathy was determined to show me the best of Belize, and to do that we had to go underwater.

The water taxi was waiting at the end of Cathy's dock to take us to the famous Shark Ray Alley—a must-see site for snorkelers and scuba divers. Once there, my fins and mask secured, I plunged in, not quite prepared for the beauty that awaited me.

It was truly the most incredible underwater experience I have ever had. I swam with giant stingrays and turtles and saw the biggest groupers I've ever seen. There were colorful rainbow fish, barracudas and sharks. Lots of sharks! Most of them were nurse sharks, known for being pretty mellow around humans, thank goodness. I got to pet one of the giant spotted stingrays, and it brushed my shoulder with its wings. It felt so soft, like a kiss on the shoulder.

As glorious as all this was, I felt numb, but fearless. I was reminded again, as I had been on my scary hike down the mountain, that nothing could really scare a person after a heartbreak, because no physical pain—not even a shark bite—is worse than the pain of a bleeding heart.

JOURNAL ENTRY
MARCH 4, 2012, BELIZE

"Heal me, O Lord, and I shall be healed; save me, and I shall be saved, for You are my praise" (Jer. 17:14).

*Save (*Yah-shah*)—to rescue, defend, to free, preserve, avenge, deliver, help.*

JOURNAL ENTRY
MARCH 5, 2012, BELIZE

Yesterday I took a small stone I found on the beach, and Cathy and I walked to a pier near her house. The stone represented all the pain, the rejection, the lies of the enemy, the grief and sorrow and tears. I walked by faith to the end of the pier and looked up to God who sees and threw the stone as hard as I could into the water. "I'm letting go, Lord. Now do what You have promised."

Swimming with Sharks

Cathy has a habit of swimming every morning from her pier to the next pier about a quarter mile away. She says it's sort of her quiet time with the Lord. I decided to try it as well, but I waited until afternoon; six in the morning was a little early for me.

We all know that exercise releases endorphins, and I needed all the endorphins I could get. I swam as hard as I could from one pier to the next, giving it everything I had. I remember seeing people on shore staring at me, probably wondering, *Why is this woman swimming like mad?*

When I arrived, breathless, at the other pier, I saw a dark patch in the clear turquoise water. It looked like a long patch of seaweed but resembled the shape of a shark. *That's odd*, I thought. Suddenly I thought the dark patch moved, and I got spooked and jumped onto the pier. As I looked down, I convinced myself it was only seaweed, so I jumped back into the water and put my head under to see if I could get a better look. Everything was blurry from the salt water, so I couldn't really tell. I thought about putting my foot on the patch to confirm that it was seaweed, but then I thought I saw it move again. Spooked again, I jumped back onto the pier and decided to watch the dark patch for a minute or so.

As I was about to get back in the water, what I thought had been a dark patch of seaweed suddenly came off the bottom and started swimming away. It was, in fact, a six-foot-long nurse shark! And I had almost put my foot on it!

I ran to the pier attendant to tell him about my shark sighting. He laughed and said, "Oh, he hangs out there all the time. He's harmless, like a big catfish." Well, apparently the shark wasn't interested in me, or he would have taken a bite while I was getting in and out of the water trying to figure out if he really was a shark. And since I didn't want to walk back to Cathy's in my soaking wet swimsuit, I decided to take the attendant's word for it.

I dove back in and swam as fast as I could to Cathy's pier. Again, I wasn't really afraid. Somehow, the experience made me feel alive, and I needed that more than ever.

JOURNAL ENTRY
MARCH 7, 2012, MORNING, BELIZE

Dear heavenly Father,

Help me to trust You again like a little girl trusts her daddy. Father, You wouldn't take something good away without giving me something better. Help me to believe that You are good and that Your mercies are new each morning.

"Rest in the LORD, *and wait patiently for Him. . . . Cease from anger and forsake wrath; do not fret—it only causes harm" (Ps. 37:7-8).*

JOURNAL ENTRY
MARCH 7, 2012, EVENING, BELIZE

My Father, My Father, where are You? Please deliver me from these tears and this pain or help me to embrace it and go through it. Father, please help me to see what You see. Let me see, Lord!

I heard You tell me that You're setting me on a new course; what is it, Lord?

A New Course

That night Cathy and I decided to take a late-night walk on the beach. We walked for miles in the soft sand up the coast of San Pedro. It was windy, and we wrapped our sarongs snuggly around our shoulders as we walked and talked. Suddenly, a voice yelled out in the dark, "Cathy!"

It was Shelley, a lady that Cathy knew from church. I had met Shelley briefly earlier in the week at a local shop. She was a beautiful woman, probably in her early 60s, and full of life. She was clearly a believer. She invited us into her beach front home, and as we chatted, our topic of conversation got around to the reason I was in Belize—trying to get over a man.

Shelley told me a story. She and her husband had been missionaries in a foreign country. They had done everything they knew to do to help a certain group of Christians there. They had loved them, given them their time and resources and poured out their lives to them for many years. But in the end the church rejected them and their biblical teachings, and went back to doing things the way they had before the missionaries had come. *What a colossal waste,* Shelley thought. She and her husband were heartbroken. She asked the Lord, "Why? What happened?" And the Lord simply told her, "Shelley, they had you; they rejected you; now move on!"

Shelley looked at me and said, "Wendy, I believe that's the word of the Lord for you too. He had you; he rejected you; now move on!"

I knew she was right, but it wasn't what I wanted to hear. I guess in my heart I was still hoping for a resurrection of my relationship with Michael.

The next day, however, I woke up feeling hope for the first time since the breakup. In fact, it turned out to be the best day I had in Belize. I got up early and put on my sundress and straw hat and walked to a little breakfast place on the water. The morning sun felt perfect as I propped my feet, with their freshly blue-painted toenails, in one chair and leaned back in another. As I sipped my coffee, I watched the morning sunlight dance on the waves, and I suddenly realized that after a week in Belize, I finally felt as if I were on vacation instead of mourning over a grave.

Some native Belizean boys approached my table smiling and showcasing their necklaces made from local stones. They were so cute that I had to buy a necklace, and I selected a jade-colored cross, the same color as the ocean. I felt light, free, and to my surprise, even a little bit happy. I also now had a clear word from the Lord: "Move on!" It was definitely a start in the right direction. Perhaps I was making progress.

On March 9 Cathy and I visited the small tropical island of Caye Caulker, about 30 minutes by boat from San Pedro. We had signed up for an all-day snorkeling adventure that included stops on several secluded islands. None of these islands had bathrooms or even outhouses, which made for interesting efforts to hide behind palm trees. We had a long day of riding in choppy water, and I was grateful when our boat finally docked again on Caye Caulker.

Sunburned and tired, I had only a few minutes to dart into a local art store, when I saw it: a large original acrylic of two colorful toucan birds. The colors were so bright; their yellow faces with teal, orange and pink beaks spoke to me. It was happy, and I needed happy in my life. The painting is now on the wall in my kitchen and a constant reminder of my precious time in beautiful Belize.

On my last day in the country, Cathy and I rode our bikes up the beautiful north shore of San Pedro. As the hot Central American sun beat down on us, I remember chanting Romans 8:28 over and over: "And we know that all things work together for good to those who love God, to those who are the called according to His purpose."

I remember that it was truly an act of faith to recite that Scripture, because I could not see at all how this breakup was going to work out for my good. But then faith is believing what we cannot see.

Cathy and I stopped for a fresh banana smoothie, which was heavenly, and that night, more sunburned than I've been in years, we ate wild-caught grouper and sipped fresh watermelon juice as we relived our day-long biking adventure. My goal in Belize had been to get healthier and happier. I had definitely gotten healthier after all the swimming, snorkeling, biking and walking. But happier? Not yet. Oh, how I wanted to leave my broken heart on the bottom of the sea. I had hoped that throwing that stone into the ocean would have somehow released my pain and relentless feelings of rejection. And even though the Lord was speaking to me and confirming my worth, I still felt betrayed and as if, somehow, I wasn't enough.

Good-bye, Shark

The morning before I left Belize, I walked out onto Cathy's pier for one last look at the sea. On that day the turquoise water was calm, and I could see the white sand on the ocean floor. It was then that I saw my shark friend. He had a huge catfish-like head with a long, sleek shark body, and he seemed to be looking up at me. I was certain that it was the same shark I had seen the other day. I can't explain it, but seeing him brought tears to my eyes. I knew that the Lord had brought the shark back to say good-bye.

We had swum together daily from pier to pier for almost two weeks (unknowingly to me most of the time, of course). Could a shark feel the pain of a human? Probably not. But somehow I felt as if he knew my heartache and wanted to tell me, *I'm going to miss you; you're stronger than you know.* Yes, I was discovering that I was braver and stronger than I knew, but I wasn't out of the seeweed yet.

I boarded my plane home with my painting and the best tan I'd had in years. On the outside I looked the picture of radiant health, but unfortunately, I flew back to Virginia Beach with my heart still broken and facing more weeks of tears than I could have possibly imagined.

I needed to "belize" that this season of tears would soon end.

REFLECTIONS

1. Have you ever felt as if you needed to escape after a breakup? Where did you go? Did it help?
2. Why is it important to take extra care of your body and your health during heartache?
3. What is it about having our heart broken that can make us feel fearless in certain situations?

6

THE "THROW UP" FACTOR

As a dog returns to his own vomit, so a fool repeats his folly.
PROVERBS 26:11

Although still heartbroken, somehow I had managed to survive until mid-April when I got this email from Michael: "I miss you, can I come and see you this weekend." I was torn. I didn't want to respond, but I so desperately missed him. And this email was different—straight, to the point, no ambiguity about how he was feeling. He missed me. It felt good—no, it felt great. Fortunately, I had an alibi, I was going to be away in New York all weekend. I didn't want to seem desperate. We talked on the phone for three hours that night; He told me how sorry he was for hurting me. He listened as I let 2 ½ months of questions and pain roll out. While in New York, he continued to email me telling me how he never wanted to hurt me or anyone like that again. I easily forgave him. Being the romantic that I was, I couldn't resist letting him meet me at the airport—it would be like old times.

I told myself that he had seen the light and that he couldn't live without me. But the Holy Spirit was whispering something much different to me: "Don't be like a dog and return to your vomit!" Really? How could this reunion be equated to something as nasty as vomit? God was about to make His point.

As I entered a stall in the ladies' room in New York's LaGuardia Airport, the woman next to me was throwing up. It is a large airport bathroom with probably 100 stalls, and somehow I selected one directly beside this unfortunate woman. Then a few hours later, during my connection in Philadelphia, where I also visited the ladies' room, I again found myself in a stall beside the sounds (and smells) of a terribly sick vomiting traveler.

God is creative and will go to great lengths to get our attention, but yours truly was not listening—yet.

When I got off the plane in Norfolk, Virginia, there he stood, looking as handsome as ever. We kissed and embraced. Everything felt so right again during those initial moments in the airport, and as we drove away together toward the beach, laughing and joking, I couldn't have felt any better. It was so good to see him again. As he drove, I turned and smiled at him just as I used to do. For a brief moment it felt as if nothing had changed, and the last two and a half months of tears and heartache suddenly seemed to have been a horrible foggy dream.

An hour later, the unseasonably warm April sun shining down on us, we talked and gazed at the ocean while leaning against the rail on the boardwalk. That's when Michael's statement hit me as hard as any wave could have: "I know I should be showing up here with a ring, but something is holding me back."

I stood silent for a few moments before saying anything. Finally, I said, "You drove three hours to meet me at the airport to tell me the same thing you told me in January—that you love me but . . . ?"

I might as well have been back in an airport stall, because I had just been thrown up on! Yuck!

It actually got worse after his first statement when he went on to tell me all the things that were wrong with me. The list was long: I wasn't funny enough (he wanted someone who made him laugh more), I wasn't tech savvy enough (I didn't have an iPhone yet—I do now!), I was too emotionally healthy (I'm not kidding), and—here's the best one—I wasn't creating enough of a chase for him. He said that he was used to girls whom he had to run after, girls who kept him on his toes. This statement from a grown man in his 40s (not a middle-school student) who ironically had driven three hours to watch me get off a plane. I was continually hurled upon with each word from his mouth.

But this should not have been a surprise to me; after all, God had warned me, "Don't be like a dog and return to your vomit."

And now I'm warning you.

You, my darling sister, are too valuable, too beautiful and too blessed to let any man throw up on you. If what's coming out of a man's mouth is not lifting you up, is not edifying and encouraging you, is not ultimately making you feel better but instead pulling you down and making you feel worse, then you are being thrown up on too.

Vomit is gross, it's disgusting, it stinks, it's nasty, and you don't want it anywhere near you, much less on you. And the Scripture says that only a fool will go back to it. Ouch! That's what I call tough love! But let's face the truth: Sometimes a woman (myself included) will ignore the stench and foulness of the vomit being spewed upon her by a man because of the one carefully placed compliment he gives or the way he smelled one time when he embraced you or the way he made you feel in that moment way back when . . . *Snap out of it!*

Just say no to vomit! God has a prince for you who would never dream of regurgitating the contents of his twisted, selfish, double-minded and dangerous heart all over you.

You, daughter of the Most High King, are a prize to be won! Never settle for vomit!

Prayer

Oh, Father, the enemy is so clever and can sometimes tempt us to return to our own "vomit" in search of something or someone who can never deliver what we really want or need. Father, please protect us and don't let Your daughters be deceived. Father, wash us from all the lies, filth, insults and hurtful words that the enemy has tried to put on us. Let us see ourselves the way You see us, as spotless, fearless, beautiful and strong and as a prize to be won! In Jesus' name, amen!

REFLECTIONS

1. Have you ever had God speak to you about a relationship through a set of circumstances—as He spoke to me through the women throwing up in the airports?
2. Why can it be difficult to trust God even when He's making it decidedly clear that a certain person is not good for you?

7

DOUBLE-MINDED WAYS

For let not that man suppose that he will receive anything from the Lord;
he is a double-minded man, unstable in all his ways.
JAMES 1:7-8

After the incident on the boardwalk in Virginia Beach, I was ready to put this relationship behind me—or so I desperately wanted to believe. Although Michael started emailing and calling me again, I knew in my spirit that he hadn't changed.

I penned the following words to Michael in an email dated April 17, 2011:

SUBJECT LINE: GOOD-BYE

Sunday (on the boardwalk) was good in that I now know the full extent of your double-mindedness, and it has helped me to fall out of love with you. Not only that, but I was having doubts too. I think I was more in love with a fantasy than a reality. Like we said in January, God has blessings for us on the other side of obedience; let's not miss the great things God is about to do.

Take care, friend,
Wendy

The Abu Sayyaf

With my personal life finally neatly put away (as I thought), I boarded a plane on April 26, 2012, for the Philippines. I hadn't been to the country in 10 years, and I was excited. I was putting Michael behind me and moving on.

I was on my way to do a 10-year-anniversary story on the kidnapping of American missionaries Martin and Gracia Burnham, a story near and dear to my heart. Not only that, but I couldn't wait to see my good friend and the producer from our Manila office, Lucille Talusan. She and I had become quite close when I had first covered the Burnhams' story 10 years ago.

In 2001 the Burnhams had been kidnapped by the notorious Abu Sayyaf—a militant Muslim group that kidnapped and often beheaded people in their vicious quest to form an independent Muslim state in the southern islands—and were held for about a year. Unfortunately, during a rescue attempt in June 2002, Martin Burnham was killed. Gracia was shot in the leg but recovered. A year after her rescue, I had been blessed to do an in-depth interview with Gracia, who had not only survived 12 months in the jungle but had amazingly said that she would do it all over again! She said nothing could compare to the intimacy she had experienced with the Lord and she wouldn't trade it for anything. Now I was privileged to be going to see her again.

Going into Abu Sayyaf territory was dangerous, and that's precisely why I liked doing it. I enjoyed the excitement of knowing that apart from God's protection, my team and I could be kidnapped as well. My white face, of course, was hard to hide in a sea of Filipinos. The last time I had landed in the southern Philippines, an airport attendant had told Lucille, "Your friend is going to be kidnapped." Lucille had had a few choice words for the young man, and she and I fervently prayed against any danger.

This time the stakes were just as high, but I had the peace of God, knowing that I was exactly where I was supposed to be. In addition to the Lord's protection, the mayor of the small town of Lamitan on Basilan Island, where we stayed, had assigned several armed body guards to me, Lucille and our cameramen. These guards were all members of the Philippine National Army, and they and their AK-47s watched over us constantly. We were treated like royalty. They even roasted a pig in our honor. I never wanted to leave.

As I had experienced on my scary hike down the mountain, God once again helped me to feel alive by putting me in a place of possible danger in which I had to use all my senses, physically and spiritually, and to depend on Him for every move. It was thrilling, and to this day my two trips to the Philippines remain my most beloved among all the international trips I've taken with CBN.

Double-Minded Ways

After we left the excitement and potential dangers of the jungles on Basilan Island, we retreated into the Mountains of Mindanao for a few days of rest and relaxation. I had my first zip-line experience, and we hung out at a camp in the mountains where we drank coffee and dined on eggs and salted dried fish for breakfast. It was delicious.

Lucille and I had been inseparable for most of the trip, but that morning she needed to go into town for an interview. I was left alone at the camp, and with the adrenaline of the last few days wearing off, I suddenly and without warning began to think about Michael.

A sudden pain gripped my heart. I missed him terribly. I started romanticizing and wondering, *If I had been kidnapped, would Michael have tried to come and rescue me?* I knew that I had sent him that good-bye letter and that it had been so strong and so right—he *had* been double-minded. But who was being double-minded now! In my weakened state my flesh and emotions took over. I had to talk to him.

Perhaps if Lucille had been there, she could have stopped me, but I was alone. I dialed his number. I hoped my voice wouldn't seem desperate, but I'm sure it did. I got his voicemail. "Hi, it's Michael. Leave a message."

"Michael, it's Wendy. I'm in the Philippines. There's something about being on the other side of the world that makes me think about the people who are important to me. I just wanted to hear your voice. Bye."

He made me wait 24 hours for his email reply.

"Hi, where are you in the Philippines? You're important to me too."

Home Sweet Home

The email exchanges, although short and sweet, continued until I got home from the Philippines. I don't know why my feelings had resurfaced so strongly, but I needed to see him. I put logic, reason, my pride and even perhaps obedience to what I believed the Lord wanted aside. I wanted to see Michael. I had taken some time off work to recover from jet lag, but I didn't need to rest. I decided to surprise him.

Michael lived three hours from me, and his home just so happened to be on the way to my mom and dad's beach home in South Carolina. I was getting ready to drive there for Mother's Day—a perfect excuse to stop by and see Michael. I would be in the neighborhood, just passing through. Yeah, right. But I didn't care. I was on a mission, and nothing could stop me, not even the song by worship leader Israel Houghton that I kept hearing on the radio:

I'm not going back, I'm moving ahead,
Here to declare to you my past is over. [1]

Annoyed at the song, I kept changing the radio dial, but it landed over and over on the convicting lyrics, "Not going back . . . moving, moving forward." The Holy Spirit was obviously trying to talk to me. "Wendy, what are you doing? You're going back to your 'vomit' again. You know you don't want the same things; he's not good for you. It's not too late—turn around; you're headed in the wrong direction!"

But sometimes a girl is gonna do what a girl is gonna do, and this girl was determined.

It was Friday morning. Michael and I hadn't exchanged any emails since I had arrived back in the country. He would definitely be surprised, and I couldn't wait to see the look on his face. We hadn't seen each other since that disappointing day on the beach, but for whatever reason—I think it's called stupidity—I wasn't thinking about that. I wanted to see him.

It's true what they say about love—it really is blind. And when you are in love, you have an amazing capacity to forgive. I forgave Michael for everything and for every time he had hurt me. I didn't know what was about to happen, but I knew that God would somehow rescue me if what I was doing was not His will.

I walked into the building where Michael worked and peeked around the corner into his office. He was surrounded by several guys, and they were talking about a project. He saw me out of the corner of his eye but didn't get up right away. I think he was trying to be cool around his fellas. When the guys left the room, Michael got up and, smiling for the first time, said, "You're here."

"Yes," I said. "I was in the neighborhood, passing through."

We hugged, and I could tell that he was glad I was there, even though it was more than a little awkward with me just showing up the way that I had. After some small talk, the two of us went to lunch, and Michael confessed how upset he had been about the email in which I had accused him of being double-minded. He told me how much those words had hurt him.

"But they were true," I said. "And now I'm the one being doubled-minded, so we're even." I hoped he would see some humor in the situation. I couldn't help smiling inside, thinking that maybe he had felt at least a fraction of the pain that I'd been feeling over the last few months.

That night Michael took me to one of our favorite outdoor restaurants. There was a wait, so we stood outside. It was chilly, so we held each other. I stroked his face, and a tear rolled down his cheek. He had missed me. It felt good to be in his arms again.

It felt even better not to be in pain. I didn't want this night to end. I didn't want to go to Myrtle Beach; I wanted to stay here forever.

Michael kissed me that night as he'd never kissed me before. Was it love, or was it merely two former lovers (who had never actually had sex) reliving old times? We talked that night about playing things by ear and not putting any pressure on ourselves to define what this was or wasn't. I tried to act as if I didn't need a commitment and didn't even want one. The truth is, though, that I was still in so much pain from the breakup that this "bandage," even if temporary, was like life-giving oxygen to someone on the top of Mount Everest gasping for air. I needed this break from the pain, even if I had to lie to Michael and to myself that I didn't want or need anything more.

Oh God, please forgive me. I can't handle this pain right now. I know that You have more for me, and I know that I probably shouldn't be here, but I so need a break from this heartache. Please put everything back the way it was. Please, Lord.

The next three weekends in a row, Michael drove to Virginia Beach to see me. On one of those weekends, as he sat on my couch typing on his laptop, he suddenly looked up and said, "My parents love you; why don't *they* marry you?" I looked up at him from where I was sitting on the other side of the room. I thought to myself, *Wendy, what are you doing? You're wasting time with a guy who is clearly making it known that he doesn't want to marry you.* "For out of the abundance of the heart his mouth speaks" (Luke 6:45).

A week later, I visited some girlfriends in New York City. Denise and Wendy and I were in Little Italy, enjoying some great pasta as we dined alfresco under the strings of twinkling lights. As the three of us shared a decadent tiramisu, I gave them an update on my situation with Michael.

Their faces said it all—they were shocked and appalled. "What are you still doing with him? You are worth so much more than that!" they almost shouted. "Break up with him now! Stop hurting yourself." Wendy, who knows about my love-hate relationship with coffee (I love it, but it doesn't love me), poignantly told me, "Michael is like coffee to you. This relationship tastes great going down, but then it comes back to bite you every time. Just say no."

As it turns out, my struggle to give up Michael was as tough, maybe tougher, than my struggle to give up coffee. Why do I love things that are bad for me?

But "I sought the LORD, and He heard me, and delivered me from all my fears" (Ps. 34:4). And after six weeks of seeing each other again, I acknowledged that my friends and the Holy Spirit were right. Michael was not good for me.

That night I called Michael from New York and told him that I didn't think I could do what we were doing anymore. "You want all the benefits of a girlfriend without a commitment," I told him. "You want someone to pray with, someone to kiss, someone to go to church with, someone to hang out with, but when I asked you what our status was—if you considered us back together—you couldn't even commit to saying that we were dating again. I can't give my kisses away for free anymore. I deserve more. I know I deserve more."

I hoped that I really believed all I was saying. Michael agreed with me, and just like that, it was over—again.

REFLECTIONS

1. Have you ever been double-minded when it comes to love?
2. What does the Bible say about being double-minded?
3. Why should you be wary of a double-minded man?

8

KANSAS CITY, HERE I COME!

Blessed is the man whose strength is in You,
whose heart is set on pilgrimage.
PSALM 84:5

After my phone call to Michael from New York in which we had ended our relationship again, I decided to take a week off from work. It was a last-minute decision but a smart one. I needed to be in the Lord's presence. I needed to hear His voice, not my own or anyone else's.

There was only one place I could think of to go: the International House of Prayer in Kansas City, Missouri. Founded by Evangelical Christian leader Mike Bickle in 1999, IHOP-KC has provided a place of 24-7 worship and prayer to anyone willing to make the pilgrimage to Kansas City. The ministry also streams its worship services online to a global audience. I couldn't wait to be in that environment—just me and the Lord and the music and the Word of God. I don't believe that time heals broken hearts—I believe that God heals broken hearts. And I needed a healing touch from God.

The next day I flew to Kansas City, hopeful but hurting. I rented a car and drove to my friend Janie's house, about 40 minutes from

IHOP. Janie and her husband and their precious daughter Hannah, graciously opened their home to me so that I could visit IHOP every day.

For the next five days, I spent as much time as I could in the prayer room, worshiping, journaling and letting the music and the presence of the Lord wash over me. My tears flowed freely as the music ministered to my soul. My situation was not unlike someone receiving medical treatment. When someone breaks an arm or a leg, he or she is rushed to the emergency room, where doctors and nurses work tirelessly to fix the broken limb. I too was broken, but my wounds were on the inside. My heart was badly shattered, and I was unable to fix it on my own. I knew that I was in the right place—a place of healing, a place of deliverance, a place of hope, and a place in which the Word of God and worship never stopped. "**Holy, Holy, Holy is the LORD Almighty; the whole earth is full of his glory**" (Isa. 6:3, *NIV*).

I was turning my eyes to Him! He was not only my Lord and Savior but my healer! Not only the great I AM, but the lover of my soul who truly did love me! Wow, what a concept—the God of the whole universe loved me! And He cared about my broken heart and had brought me here to His "hospital," where fellow Christians and angels I couldn't see were ministering to my soul. I would not die but live and would declare the works of the Lord (see Ps. 118:17)! Hallelujah! This place was as close to heaven as I could get without actually going there, and although I was badly wounded, I wasn't ready to go to heaven yet—I just needed to be healed and get back on the front lines.

JOURNAL ENTRY
JUNE 19, 2012, KANSAS CITY, MISSOURI

Father, I'm here! This is where my soul longs to be. "The LORD is near to those who have a broken heart, and saves such as have a contrite spirit" (Ps. 34:18).

Lord, I come to You broken, broken in so many ways—my heart, my body, my soul, my spirit. You are near! Consume me, Lord, with Your fiery, healing, cleansing love.

Lord, operate on my heart! Remove my passion for Michael if he's not Your will for me—please take it, Lord!

I felt the Lord speak back to my spirit: "I know how hard this is for you, Wendy. I feel your heartbreak, daughter. Give your tears to Me. I will give you hope, Wendy; I will give you hope and no more sorrow."

Great Is Your Reward

And then I heard the Lord say this: "Rejoice, daughter, for great is your reward for your obedience."

Obedience, Lord? This doesn't feel like obedience, but maybe it is.

I had a choice to stay in my relationship with Michael as it was, on his terms with no commitment, but I knew the Holy Spirit was calling me to something greater. He was telling me that although this was the most painful thing I had ever experienced and it didn't make sense right now, if I simply obeyed Him, trusted Him with my heart, trusted Him to lead me out, I would be rewarded.

I continued to journal:

I will obey You, Lord. I will trust You with joy; I will surrender my life to You. My hope is in You, Lord! I have nothing without You. I offer to You all that I am—all that You've given me! Use me, Lord! I give You my dream to be married, Lord.

"Search from the book of the LORD, and read: Not one of these shall fail; not one shall lack her mate. For My mouth has commanded it, and His Spirit has gathered them" (Isa. 34:16).

There is a coffee shop next to IHOP's prayer room where people gather to refuel and to re-caffeinate between worship sets. I was sitting at a table with my new friend Silvy from India, who was also staying with Janie. At a neighboring table was a man I recognized from the prayer room who had been walking the perimeter of the room and praying intensely for what seemed like hours. Now he was sitting right next to us, praying for people as they came over to his table in the coffee shop. We smiled and asked, "Are you praying for everyone?"

He smiled back and asked if he could join us.

"Sure," we said.

The man's name was Anthony, and he was what I call a prayer warrior. A few minutes into our conversation, I realized that my heart had stopped hurting. Seeing Anthony's David-like warrior spirit was inspiring me to believe that God had a man for me who had this kind of spirit! I was amazed, as I listened to him talk, at how my heart leapt with excitement. Anthony was passionate about the things of God, and his eyes lit up when he talked. I knew that deep down this was the kind of man I wanted. Someone with this zeal, passion and spiritual strength! After listening to my story, Anthony told me, "You and Michael were unequally yoked, but God has the right one for you, and he'll be worth the wait."

JOURNAL ENTRY
JUNE 20, 2012, KANSAS CITY, MISSOURI

I knew in my spirit that what Anthony said was true—but this morning, I still miss Michael's emails.

Oh, the pain of doing things my own way, of not waiting on the Lord, of not trusting His goodness and of thinking I knew what I was doing when I did not. But last night God stepped into my pain and gave me relief through Anthony—through his passion and prayers, I felt alive and ready to trust God again. Thank You, Lord, and thank you, Anthony, wherever you are.

Psalm 119:116: "Uphold me according to your word, that I may live; and do not let me be ashamed of my hope."

As I was bringing my broken heart daily to God's altar at IHOP-KC, I was also devouring Elisabeth Elliot's book *Quest for Love*. My friend

Janie had loaned it to me, and I couldn't put it down. How I wished that I'd read it before my heartbreak. But Elliot makes the case that a broken heart is a precious thing to God.

"A broken heart is an acceptable offering to God. He will never despise it. We do not know what unimagined good He can bring about through our simple offering."[1] She goes on to say that God has a "glorious purpose in permitting the heartbreak." Could that be true? Perhaps when it doesn't hurt so badly, I might be able to believe that, I hoped.

Cheesecake vs. Jell-O® Pudding

As my week at IHOP went on, I heard a sermon that put a whole new perspective on my situation. The preacher told the crowd that when he was growing up, one of his favorite desserts was cheesecake. From the time he could remember until he was in high school, he and his family had enjoyed cheesecake regularly. His mother always made Jell-O® pudding cheesecake—light, airy and fluffy.

But when this man was about 17, he took his first trip to New York City, where he took his first bite of real New York cheesecake, and lo and behold—he became furious! His whole life he had been eating an inferior cheesecake and had never known that New York cheesecake even existed. He could never settle again for the fluffy Jell-O® pudding version that he had grown up on. From that day on it was the rich, creamy and decadent New York cheesecake for him or none at all! "I was angry that I had settled for a lesser pleasure," he said.

His point was that sometimes in life we simply don't know what we're missing because of our ignorance. Other times we need God to radically change our palate so that we will desire the real thing, not a "Jell-O® pudding" version of the real thing. I knew the Lord was speaking to me: He had the real "cheesecake" for me! He had a superior pleasure for me, not an inferior one. But first I needed to change my palate.

"A person with an expensive palate only likes high-priced culinary treats. Someone who tastes slight nuances in food is said to have a well-developed palate, and someone who only likes fancy food is said to have a sophisticated palate."[2] I definitely needed a palate upgrade. I was used to surviving on crumbs.

I was reminded of the fact that Michael had been making a half-hearted effort to win my heart, when I knew that I was worth more. Just as the preacher hadn't been willing to settle for Jell-O® pudding cheesecake anymore, I wasn't going to settle for a halfhearted relationship anymore.

Still, changing my palate and my desires would be hard work, especially after I had invested so much of my heart into a "Jello® cheesecake" relationship. I still struggled to let go.

JOURNAL ENTRY
JUNE 21, 2012, KANSAS CITY, MISSOURI

The pain I'm feeling right now is worse than the pain I had when I was in the relationship and knew that something was wrong. This pain feels like someone took all the air out of my lungs or punched me really hard in the stomach. I know that it's for the best; I know that God is with me; I know that God has "best" for me—not a counterfeit, not almost right, not, "I love you but . . ." Father, only You in Your greatness, in Your great love for me, can heal my heart and soul. Lord, You saw what was coming. Lord, help me desire Your best now. Help me forgive freely and completely in Jesus' name. Today I walk away from the good so that I can receive and experience God's best for me. I trust God with my future. He will give me the desires of my heart. Give me strength, oh God! Give me strength.

"I trust in You, O LORD; I say, 'You are my God.' My times are in your hand" (Ps. 31:14-15).

Looking back, I can see that my time at IHOP was invaluable in my healing process. If you're going through heartbreak, remember that there's no one who understands your pain more than Jesus does.

He not only suffered incredible torture on the cross but also unfathomable rejection from His own people. He knows what a broken heart feels like, and He feels your pain.

Jesus cares. Taking a pilgrimage to sit at His feet for a week was the smartest thing I could have done. Was I healed instantly? No. But I received strength, encouragement and hope for the next phase of my journey toward wholeness. The Bible says, "In Your presence is fullness of joy" (Ps. 16:11).

It's funny how it took heartbreak to make me so desperate to find the Lord that I hopped on a plane and took off for Kansas City. How I long for more times like I had there—where my only focus was on sitting at God's feet, meditating on His Word, and worshiping the One who is worthy of all my praise. I have found this to be true: There is no relationship on earth that will ever satisfy your soul like your relationship with Jesus.

Prayer

Lord, You are the lover of our souls. We long to be with You, to know You intimately and to hear Your sweet, soft voice. No one and nothing can satisfy us the way You do. Lord, help us to run to You for our healing. Like a deer pants for water, so our soul thirsts for You, Lord. Father, I lift up every precious heart reading this that desperately needs Your healing touch, pour out Your oil of gladness. Revive us again, Refresh us, Lord. Give us hope, Lord, for the glorious future that still awaits us. In Jesus' glorious name, amen.

REFLECTIONS

1. Why is it so important to seek the Lord and to hear His voice during and after a relationship?
2. Has God ever asked you to give up a relationship? Were you obedient?
3. Have you ever settled for "Jell-O® cheesecake" instead of waiting on God for the real "New York cheesecake"?

9

YOU ARE A PRIZE TO BE WON!

The kingdom of heaven is like a merchant seeking beautiful pearls,
who, when he had found one pearl of great price,
went and sold all that he had and bought it.
MATTHEW 13:45-46

I would love to tell you that after my week at IHOP-KC, I was as good as new. Unfortunately, that was not the case. Although I was somewhat renewed in my spirit, my heartache was still present—I woke up with it and went to bed with it. How I wanted it to leave already! But apparently there was no clear ending point to this pain, and I would have to trust God to get me through.

The summer dragged on, but in mid-July—a small ray of hope. I had forced myself to go to an amusement park with some girlfriends in hopes of being amused, and I was standing in the rain listening to a Christian rock band when I heard the Holy Spirit say to my heart, "This season will end!" Hallelujah! My tears, mixed with rain drops, poured down my face. *Thank You, Father. I really needed to hear that.*

One of the most painful lessons that I was now learning is that I did not really know my true value. Because of that, I had become the "beggar" in my relationship with Michael, begging for a few crumbs of love when God had so much more for me!

As I pondered these things in my heart, I was reminded of something the Lord had spoken to me several years before, something that I believed was true and had even preached to other women but had not taken to heart.

I had been in Florida covering Terry Schiavo's right-to-life case, one of the biggest stories of 2005. All the national media were there. After a long day of filming, I did something I normally don't do. I asked a guy who was closely involved with the story and with whom I'd been working all day if he'd like to go out to dinner. He was my age, handsome and a single Christian like I was, and after a whirlwind day of interviews and a few laughs, I rationalized that it would be fine to ask him to have dinner with me instead of dining alone. His response was not what I had been expecting: "I have to go to the gym."

I felt sick! It was as if someone had punched me in the stomach. Why had I done that? I had known better, but we had seemed to be getting along so well. But isn't that lesson in Dating 101? Never ask a guy out! Discouraged and a little mad at myself, I drove back to the hotel alone, when suddenly I heard the unmistakable voice of the Lord in my spirit. He whispered so clearly to me, *Wendy, you are a prize to be won!*

I knew the Lord's voice, and I knew that He was speaking to me about my value. I didn't need to be the one pursuing a relationship or running around like a chicken with my head cut off, looking for love in all the wrong places. God has my man, and that man is going to recognize me as his prize! And the same goes for you.

Unfortunately, I have had to learn this lesson the hard way.

Pearl of Great Price

Ladies, the Lord wants you to know that you are a pearl of great price, a treasure worth pursuing and protecting. You are worth fighting for and, like the pearl in the parable at the head of this chapter, worth everything it might cost a guy to obtain you. You are worth someone sacrificing his time, his routine, his comfort, his money, his whatever in order to have you. You are worth it! You are a prize to be won. Don't settle for crumbs.

Several months after my relationship with Michael was truly over, I was attending a formal dinner at one of our CBN partner events. As I finished my dessert, one of our partners, a tall, lanky blond-haired man whom I had never laid eyes on, approached me and said, "I've been praying for you." Then he told me, "The Lord gave me a word for you." Intrigued to say the least, I asked this man, "Really? What is it?" *"Pearl of great price!"* he said with a look of compassion.

My eyes flooded with tears. The man went on, "I saw you this time last year with a certain gentleman"—that would have been Michael—"and the Holy Spirit told me, 'He is not the one for her, because *he is not willing to pay the price for the pearl of great price!*'" More tears. Wow, this was a much needed word, and at exactly the right time, as this was my birthday weekend, and I was really missing having someone special in my life.

This man finished by telling me, "The man the Lord has for you will be able to pay the price for the pearl of great price."

Ladies, isn't that what we all want—the man who is willing to pay the price for us? Not with words only but also with deeds. The man who will go the distance, walk across a desert, climb a mountain and do whatever it takes to win us.

Jacob Pays the Price for Rachel

One of the most inspiring love stories in the Bible is the story of Jacob and Rachel. In fact, it may be one of the greatest love stories of all time.

Jacob had been sent by his father Isaac to find a wife from a relative's family. He traveled a long distance to his mother's family, and when he met Rachel at a well, for him it was love at first sight. Jacob single-handedly moved the great stone cover off the well, perhaps trying to impress Rachel: "When Jacob saw Rachel, daughter of his uncle Laban, and Laban's sheep, he went over and rolled the stone away from the mouth of the well and watered his uncle's sheep. Then Jacob kissed Rachel and began to weep aloud" (Gen. 29:10-11, *NIV*).

Interestingly, it wasn't Rachel who cried but Jacob. He seemed to know with certainty that Rachel would be his bride. Rachel ran to her father and told him about the young traveler. Rachel's father, Laban, ran out to meet Jacob, and then he hugged him and kissed him and invited him to his home.

Jacob stayed with Laban's family and within a month fell deeply in love with Rachel. He was determined to marry her. But before he would allow Jacob to do so, Rachel's father convinced Jacob to work for him for seven years. Jacob agreed. Jacob was so in love with Rachel that the Bible says the time flew by: "They seemed like only a few days to him because of his love for her" (Gen. 29:20, *NIV*). Wow, talk about romantic! I'd like to see a modern romantic comedy come even close to depicting this kind of love and sacrifice.

But, ladies, take heart! I have discovered in writing this book that there are plenty of great guys out there with hearts of gold who, like Jacob, have paid the price or can't wait to pay the price for the women they love and cherish.

Modern-Day Jacobs

CBN cameraman Ben Hornby, a good friend of mine with whom I have worked for many years, tells this story of his attempt to ask for his now wife's hand in marriage:

> When I asked my future father-in-law for his daughter Jenny's hand in marriage, he said, "Before I answer, I want you to come to China with me for two weeks on a business trip." So off to China I went with Jenny's father and mother—just the three of us in one hotel room. Jenny stayed at home. Awkwardness would be a way of life for the next two weeks.

During a three-day layover in South Korea on our way to China, they left me alone for two whole days with a family that didn't speak any English. They served me octopus pizza with fish flavored crust and kimchi! I got sick and couldn't communicate with them that I needed cold and stomach medicine badly. I hardly slept a wink, because the only available bed was their eight-year-old daughter's, and only about half of my six-foot-three, 230-pound frame fit on it. I actually slept better on the floor, which is what I ended up doing.

I kept reminding myself hourly why I was doing this: *I love Jenny, and I can't live without her.* She and I didn't get to talk on the phone while I was gone, but I thought of her constantly, thinking, *If I can make it through these two weeks, I will get to spend the rest of my life with the woman of my dreams.*

Once we finally got to China, we took one three-hour bumpy ride after another to visit all of Jenny's father's friends. Through mountainous roads and rice patties, car-sickness was another cross I had to bear. I did the best I could not to let on how miserable I was, and at every spare moment I looked for an Internet cafe and emailed Jenny to let her know how much I was missing her. Once in a while I would see a McDonald's or a KFC, and they were like an oasis in the desert, although neither the food nor the service was anything like I was used to—except for that one Starbucks in Beijing. It was like heaven.

At one restaurant we had fish that actually moved on the plate before we started eating it! I about puked during one lavish dinner as I looked at piles of what looked like half-digested food all over the table. I wasn't aware that it was bad manners to discreetly dispose of these things in a napkin. Rather, it is preferred that a person spit them out in his or her hand and places them in a pile next to the plate. Without knowing I was doing it, I think I offended half of

China. Then it was back to the hotel room—our one hotel room. Jenny's dad, mom, and I in one room. Fortunately for me, I did have my own bed. Again, I reminded myself that this totally awkward situation would soon be over and that if I had the privilege of slipping that sparkling engagement ring on Jenny's finger, this would all be worth it.

When the trip finally ended, I felt pretty good about how things had gone with the three of us, so I mustered up the courage to approach Jenny's dad again to ask for her hand in marriage. But guess what? Jenny's dad still wasn't ready. He said, "I'm not there yet. I'm only 60 percent there." I was shocked and disappointed, to say the least, especially after enduring two weeks of seeing moving food and ingesting stomach medicine. I was starting to understand how Jacob had felt when he'd had to work seven years for his beloved Rachel.

I actually ended up having to ask Jenny's dad for her hand three times! Granted, every time he told me not yet, his percentage of being ready was higher. Finally, one day during a Christmas event with Jenny's family, out of the blue he tapped me on the shoulder, looked me in the eyes and said, "Ben, you passed the test. I'm 100 percent there. I'm ready for you to marry my daughter."

And there it was. I bought the ring in January, and I proposed to Jenny two days after Valentine's Day.

There wasn't much creativity to my proposal for some reason. Maybe it was because my nerves were so frayed from asking her father three times. Basically, I took her out to dinner and nonchalantly placed the ring in front of her in the middle of our dinner conversation. Jenny's reaction was priceless.

As soon as her eyes saw it, she looked up at me and shrieked and hollered, putting her hand over her mouth. She was so excited and so surprised. Hyperventilating and grinning from ear to ear, the first thing she said was, "I can't

touch it! You have to put it on!" As I gingerly placed the ring
on her finger, I asked her to marry me and she excitedly said
yes. Then, after a little more screaming, she politely asked
if she could call her friends and family to share the news.
I obliged. She and I went to the pay phone in the back of the
restaurant, and I stood beside her as she went through her
Rolodex hollering with excitement.

We were married on August 26, 2000. Jenny was definitely worth the wait.

Another male colleague of mine, Bob Womack, won his sweet-
heart with something near and dear to every girl's heart: chocolate.
Bob recalls,

While attending a Christian college that sat on the crest of a
remote Tennessee mountaintop, on a lark I asked a pretty gal
from New Jersey if she'd like to go to a local restaurant for
dessert and to study. Though she wasn't particularly interested in a southern boy like me, the meals at the school were
deplorable, and a shot at decent food was a strong incentive.
That evening, I talked more freely with Ruth than I ever had
with any girl. I found her straightforwardness totally refreshing. We talked of our mutual love for Christmas and for old
houses. When I drove her back up to school, she told me flat
out that we couldn't date because she was everything but
engaged to a boy from her hometown.

I suppose I took that as a challenge. I arranged to cross
her path at school as often as possible. I offered to take her
out "to study" again within days. Though I made only a tiny
amount of money through work study, I made excuses to
lightheartedly take her out for dinner or dessert, asking no return commitment. Ruth had no car to get off campus. I did.

Then I got her addicted to the most fantastic, scrump-
tious, sinfully rich double-chocolate fudge cake I'd ever

experienced, better than I've ever had since. If I could do nothing else, I could buy her coffee and fudge cake. I offered to show her the hiking trails on the mountain and the historical attractions in the area. Those hikes turned out to be her strongest memories of our dating days, except, of course, that fudge cake.

I had been raised to respect ladies as something special to be cherished and respected, and that was the center of my approach to the relationship. I soon came to the conclusion that Ruth was a particularly special lady and worth every effort I could invest. In a short while we were eating our meals together and getting together to pray every morning. I tried to find excuses to fill all her spare time, figuring the easiest way to be her only "dance partner" was to fill in every space on her dance card with my name, so to speak. We even shared my laundry money. Eventually she even relented and let me take her on something resembling a date.

Then she flew back to her home, 800 miles away, for fall break. Her mom wisely suggested that for fairness's sake she had to decide between her almost-engagement and me. I won! The night she returned and told me of her decision was the night I asked her for our first kiss. We began to spend our weekends together. By month three we were talking about the future.

The next year, Ruth and I were slated to attend colleges in different states, hundreds of miles apart. She'd had some recent experience with long-distance relationship and concluded that it didn't work. By the end of month four, we had to decide whether to stay together geographically for the next school year or let each other go. I had a scholarship to my next school, so there was no way I could afford to follow her. All I could do was pray. After Christmas break she gave me the good news. She had decided to abandon her plans and to follow me.

Being an honorable man, I felt that it wasn't fair for her to make a commitment that large and to disrupt her plans on my behalf without having a commitment from me. I knew that I needed to make my intentions clear. She deserved that and so much more. I spent a prayerful month settling my heart and head, and around Valentine's Day of 1979, six months in, I took her back to that first restaurant and to the first booth we had sat in. We had dinner and that famous fudge cake, and I asked her for her hand. She said yes, but wisely wouldn't allow an announcement without an engagement ring. Unfortunately, I had invested all my money in the fudge-cake market. In the next weeks I took her out shopping for a band and mount. I saved and bought the one she liked. I would continue to save for a diamond.

A month later, on spring break, we traveled to her home for me to meet her folks and to get their blessing. Her mother took us to a Christian jeweler's shop on an errand. We told the jeweler that we were at a Christian college where I was studying Bible and that we were hoping to be able to afford a diamond one day so we could announce our engagement. Could he educate us on diamonds? He taught us some alright, but then he showed us a bunch of diamonds and asked Ruth to select one that matched her dreams. She chose one, and he said, "Let's mount it." I protested that I didn't have the money and would have to save for it. He said, "Forget that! You take the ring back to school and announce your engagement. Pay me as you get the money. If you don't pay me, you aren't cheating me, you are cheating the Holy Spirit." It was my first loan. After a year of saving every penny, I indeed paid off the ring.

How did I feel about spending every cent for two years on nurturing this relationship? I was excited. I was thrilled. Frankly, I was intoxicated. Ruth was the greatest woman I'd ever spent time with. This was to be the biggest relationship in my life. She was easily worth every penny I had, *and more*. Thirty-five years later Ruth is still my best friend, and we are still madly in love. Winning my wife was a bargain, and the best exchange I ever made.

My friend and co-anchor Mark Martin also shared his amazing story of how he won his pearl of great price:

My wife and I met in college at Oral Roberts University. We were friends until spring break of 1991. That's when she and I and another couple traveled to Colorado for some leisure time in the Rocky Mountains. I had always thought of Lisa as a fun friend until our road trip to Aspen. I recall the four of us piled into a van, along with the parents and sibling of one of the friends. I don't remember what we were talking about, but whatever the content of the conversation, it caused me to look at Lisa in a different way. It was an epiphany, a magical moment. I believe the Holy Spirit dropped in my heart the thought, *She would make a great wife*. From that time forward, I pursued her romantically. That was our freshman year; we dated all four years of college.

It wasn't a storybook romance by any means; we had our share of arguments. We even broke up for three weeks at my urging. Being highly career-oriented, I wasn't sure what I wanted—a single life devoted to workplace dreams or a married life filled with happiness at home and at work. I realized, however, that while we were apart for those three weeks I missed her terribly. Our relationship was divinely orchestrated—we belonged together. She was away from campus when I tried to patch things up. I tracked her down via phone and apologized, and Lisa graciously agreed to give me a second chance.

Our relationship was so comfortable. I enjoyed her company, and she enjoyed mine. After a couple years of dating, however, Lisa needed clarification. I'll never forget the day she sat me down in the college cafeteria and wanted to know where our relationship was headed. Being somewhat of a commitment-phobe, my eyes widened when she boldly told me that if things weren't going where she thought they were going—down the path to marriage—she wanted out; there were other fish in the sea. I had this pearl in my hand but had taken her for granted. Her words jolted my thoughts and actions. I did *not* want to lose her, so it was time for me to think about marriage.

Shortly after our cafeteria conversation, I got a job as a host at a nearby restaurant so I could save money to buy Lisa an engagement ring. She had dreamed of "showing off" her ring, not boastfully but excitedly, to her friends before graduation, and I did not want to mess that up. Eventually, a ring was purchased—a half-carat diamond with a unique, tiny diamond-laced band that she picked out. In the world's eyes, it wasn't spectacular to behold, but in God's eyes it symbolized a powerful covenant.

I proposed to Lisa about a week and a half before graduation—in the nick of time. One of our best friends, Jerry, hid behind a tree at the park where Lisa and I had first met. He held a velvet-like pillow in his hands with the ring on top. Lisa and I walked near that tree, and Jerry jumped out, greeting a surprised and giddy Lisa. I got down on one knee and asked the love of my life to marry me. She joyfully accepted my proposal and wore the ring with deep contentment. We were engaged for close to eight months before tying the knot.

We've been married now for 18 and a half years. My bride is my best friend. What would have happened if we never had that cafeteria conversation? Only God knows. Thankfully to Him, I took her words to heart and didn't lose a beautiful pearl.

Jesus Is the Ultimate Example

There are many examples of men who "paid the price" for their brides, but the apostle Paul says that the greatest example of sacrificial love is Jesus: "In this the love of God was manifested toward us, that God has sent His only begotten Son into the world, that we might live through Him" (1 John 4:9).

What kind of love sacrifices its very life so that we might live? The love of Jesus does—and the Bible calls men to love their wives with that same kind of love:

> Husbands, love your wives, just as Christ also loved the church and gave Himself for her, that He might sanctify and cleanse her with the washing of water by the word, that He might present her to Himself a glorious church, not having spot or wrinkle or any such thing, but that she should be holy and without blemish. So husbands ought to love their own wives as their own bodies; *he who loves his wife loves himself* (Eph. 5:25-28, emphasis added).

There Should Never Be a "But" After "I Love You"

Ladies, one thing I know for sure: There should never be a "but" after "I love you."

Love—the kind that Jacob had for Rachel, the kind that Ben had for Jenny and especially the kind of love that Jesus had for us—would never include an escape clause. Can you imagine Jacob saying to Rachel, "I really think you're pretty, and I love you, *but* I don't know if after working for your dad I'm still going to want to marry you." Can you imagine Jesus saying to us, "I love you, *but* I'm really not sure that I can die for you. I'm really not sure that you're worth all that." Sounds pretty ridiculous doesn't it? And that's how it sounded to me too.

I remember thinking, *My boyfriend just told me that he loves me, so why doesn't it feel good? Why does my soul hurt?* It hurt because he tacked on, "But I don't know if you're 'the one.'" He was basically saying, "I love you, but I want to keep my options open. I'm not willing to pay the price for you." The truth is, I was so longing to hear those three precious words that when he finally said them but tacked on *"but I don't know if you're 'the one,'"* I was like a deer in the headlights. I didn't know what to do.

If I had a chance to do that moment over, I would look him in the eye and say, "You can take your 'but' and your butt and head on back to where you came from. I am worth much more than 'I love you but'! There should never be a 'but' after 'I love you.'"

Don't make the same mistake I did. You are a prize to be won, and so am I! You are worth fighting for. You are not only worthy of love, but you are worthy of "I love you" period. If a man can't say it straight, if he's trying to leave himself a loophole or an out clause, he isn't the one for you anyway. God has a better plan—and a better man. Never settle.

Prayer

Lord, thank You that when we know our true value, we won't settle for second best. Help us to see ourselves through Your loving eyes, as women of value, women of substance, women of beauty and women of strength who are worth fighting for, worth scaling a mountain for or crossing a desert for. Lord, You paid the ultimate price for us. You said that we were worth dying for. And because of that, we know that we are worthy of a great love. Lord, thank You that our great loves—our extravagant loves—are on the way! In Jesus' mighty name, amen.

REFLECTIONS

1. Do you see yourself as a prize to be won?
2. How do you get your self-worth—from others' opinions or from what Jesus Christ says about you?
3. Why is it impossible to "settle" when you know your true value?

10

GUARD YOUR HEART

My son [daughter], pay attention to what I say; turn your ear to my words.
Do not let them out of your sight, keep them within your heart;
for they are life to those who find them and health to one's whole body.
Above all else, guard your heart, for everything you do flows from it.
PROVERBS 4:20-23, TNIV

I never understood the importance of obeying this Scripture until I had my heart broken. "Guard your heart," the writer of this proverb pleads with us. "Above all else!" he urges. Obviously, he knew something we didn't, and he wanted to keep us from injuring ourselves. Oh, how I wish I had listened and taken his timeless warning to heart.

The *King James Version* puts Proverbs 4:23 like this: "Keep thy heart with all diligence; for out of it are the issues [or the wellspring] of life." But I think this version from the *Complete Jewish Bible* says it best: "Above everything else, guard your heart; for it is the source of life's consequences." Wow, is that ever true.

If you need further proof of how serious this command is, check out the Hebrew translation, which gives rich meaning to the phrase:

The word *mishmar* ("guard") refers to the act of guarding someone closely, just as an officer or warden might keep watch over a prisoner. The phrase translated "with all diligence" (*mikkol-mishmar*) literally means "more than anything that might be guarded," and is used here to intensify the command to guard. Plainly put, this verse commands us to watch over the heart more than anything else.

Why? Because from the heart are *totz'ot chaiyim*—the "issues" of life. . . . The word *totz'ot* is mainly used to refer to the borders of territories or the boundaries of a city. This verse is saying that from the heart of a person . . . a "map" or "chart" to life is drawn.[1]

How you choose to guard your heart from deception, corruption or hardness will determine the "road" of your life.

The Dangers of an Unguarded Heart

When I first started going out with Michael, he pursued me with such passion and enthusiasm and with what I naively assumed was love that although he never actually told me "I love you," after several months of dating him, I gave him my heart. But apparently, when he sensed I had both feet in the relationship, he started to back away, saying he wasn't sure that I was "the one." I was devastated, but by then it was too late for me to get my heart back.

He had told me earlier in the relationship that he was trying to win my heart, so I never even thought about guarding it. In fact, I remember confidently saying in response to him, "You haven't won my heart yet," and thinking that there was a fat chance he ever would. But I learned that emotions can change quickly in a relationship. Almost without warning, after a romantic night down at the beach, where we watched a wedding taking place in the sand, I remember thinking, *I could marry this man; I think I'm in love with him.* And what's worse, I told him I loved him first! So there I was, my heart totally unguarded, totally defenseless and totally clueless about the dangerous emotional road that I had just taken.

If I had only understood the gravitas of this Scripture and the painful consequences of not guarding my heart, I most certainly would have kept my mouth shut and waited until Michael had verbally professed his love for me before giving him my heart, my most prized possession.

In Elisabeth Elliot's wonderful classic book *Passion and Purity*, she urges women always to wait to express their emotions until a man makes his intentions clear.

But maybe you're saying to yourself, *But Wendy, I don't want to play games. If I love someone, I'm going to tell him.* Well, I will say this: You're taking a risk. Of course, there are always exceptions. Doing that did work for my sister JeanAnne. She told her husband-to-be that she loved him before he told her that he loved her. And today they are happily married with two beautiful children and are more in love than ever. But the general rule, if you want to guard your heart, is to wait. Wait for the man to make the first move.

After Michael and I broke up and he finally confessed to me the real reasons he hadn't wanted to continue our relationship—not the "God told me to give you back" reason—he told me, "I wanted to be the one to tell you I loved you first. When you told me first, it took all the pursuit out of the relationship." Well, we had already been together for five months, and I don't think it was my telling him that I loved him that ended the relationship. But I can't speak for him, so I may never know the real reasons. I do know this: Hearing that my saying "I love you" to him was basically a turn-off for him was—well, there are really no words that can express how painful that was to me. I felt like a fool for having given those words that meant so much to me to someone who could not receive or appreciate them. Someone, who in the end, was not worthy of receiving them.

The Heart: The Most Important Thing You Can Guard

Pastor Greg Allen of Bethany Bible Church in Portland, Oregon, says that out of all the things in life for which we are forced to take security measures, the Bible presents our heart as the most important of all:

If you effectively protect your car from theft, your home from burglary, your property from damage, your financial interests from failure, and your body from personal illness and injury, and even our borders from terrorist attacks—and yet fail in protecting this one, all-important thing as the Bible warns us—that singular failure will affect all other areas of life. The plain fact is that more personal ruin and eternal loss has been caused by a failure to protect this one thing than all failures to protect material matters combined. And yet, hardly anyone gives a single thought to "keeping the heart."[2]

The Enemy Is After Your Heart

Just as some cities have levees to keep water from coming in and ruining their streets and homes, so we must have levees (protectors) around our heart, because the enemy wants to steal it!

I was in New Orleans the night Hurricane Katrina blew through in 2005. My crew and I were huddled in one room on the seventh floor of the Hilton Hotel in downtown New Orleans. We spent a long night, feeling the hotel sway back and forth and wondering if we would survive to tell the story.

When morning broke and the storm had nearly passed, my crew and I eagerly went out to investigate. We were surprised that the wind damage to the French Quarter didn't look too bad. There were a lot of downed trees and power lines but no major damage. But then we saw it—on the other side of the interstate, the water was up to the housetops. People were on their roofs waving for help. We even saw a body floating facedown in the water. It wasn't the high winds from the category 5 monster storm that had been the worst of it—it was the levees breaking and the water pouring in (billions of gallons) from Lake Pontchartrain that had caused the real death and destruction.

The next day, we helplessly watched as another levee broke at the 17th Street Canal. I remember walking along Canal Street, talking to residents as the water rose inch by inch until it was waist deep in places.

When the levees broke, it seemed that all hell broke loose in New Orleans. The looters came out in huge numbers, breaking into stores, stealing merchandise and food and anything they could get their hands on. My cameraman had a knife pulled on him, and my crew and I had a strong and eerie sense that we needed to leave the city soon, before it was too late.

I'll never forget driving out of the city and seeing a woman walking in waist-high water, carrying her suitcase on her shoulder. Perhaps it held the most precious things that she owned or only what she could grab as quickly as possible. It's been a long road to recovery for New Orleans, but city officials vowed to strengthen the city's levees so that this kind of destruction would never happen again. I pray that the Lord will continue to rebuild the Crescent City and make sure her levees are fortified and ready for any future storms. As for the lady with the suitcase, I pray that wherever she is today, she is healthy, happy and hopefully still thanking God that she survived one of the worst natural disasters in U.S. history.

Fortify the Levees

Don't wait to fortify the levees of your heart. The enemy is sly, and he often comes to us dressed as a wolf in sheep's clothing. He desperately wants to injure, torture and even kill your heart. His goal is to get you sidetracked and hopefully to take you out of the game—if not forever, at least temporarily. He knows that if he can get your "heart"—the seat of your passions, thoughts, emotions, dreams, the matrix of who you are and everything that makes you feel alive—then he can do serious damage to you and even derail you from your destiny.

Don't let him in. When the devil comes knocking, don't answer. Don't let anyone pull the wool over your eyes! You are too important to the kingdom of God. Learn to guard your heart so that you don't end up a disaster zone like New Orleans after Hurricane Katrina. It's not easy, but it is *so* worth it!

You may not end up with the guy you're currently dating or the guy you think you're in love with right now, but if you guard your heart, keep your mouth shut and don't put all your cards on the table, you will be in a much better position when you do meet "the one," because you won't be nursing a broken heart. Guard your heart! Above all else! Guard it! Then you will stay strong and sober, and you will know God's will and the way He has for you!

Keys to Guarding Your Heart

1. Be Discerning

Don't assume that a man is in love with you if he has not verbally communicated that to you. Even a man who is affectionate and who does all the right things may be light years away from making a true commitment. In the old days, a father would ask a young suitor to state his intentions if the young man was asking his daughter out for a date. Although that approach may be somewhat outdated, your heavenly Father is still concerned about the intentions of your suitors and wants you to guard your heart until you know where a relationship is going.

If after several months a man is still not stating his intentions to you or he's giving you the "one day at a time" speech, then he's not serious about you, and you'll be glad you protected your heart. Time to move on, girlfriend. God's got something better for you.

2. Guard Your Thoughts

Don't plan your honeymoon and your wedding after the first date. Why do we girls do this? I think we're so wired from a young age to want the "fairytale" that our minds go right to the dress, the cake, the exotic honeymoon destination and yes, the guest list. I am so guilty of this. I once stopped at a resort to inquire about wedding venues, etc. and no, there was no ring on my finger and no proposal in sight. If you let your mind run ahead of you like this, you may miss the important signs or red flags that God wants you to see in the here and now.

[Bring] every thought into captivity to the obedience of Christ (2 Cor. 10:5).

Search me, O God [the idea is, Search me thoroughly; examine not merely my outward conduct, but what I think about; what are my purposes; what passes through my mind; what occupies my imagination and my memory; what secures my affections and controls my will] . . . and lead me in the way everlasting (Ps. 139:23-24 with *Barnes' Notes on the Bible* on Ps. 139:23).

3. Guard Your Speech

"Death and life are in the power of the tongue, and those who love it will eat its fruits" (Prov. 18:21). As we already heard from Elisabeth Elliot, if you don't know where you stand with a man, best to keep your lips firmly shut until he states his intentions.

But if you listen closely, a man will often let you know exactly how he feels about you in casual conversation. As I mentioned before, one day out of the blue, Michael said to me, "My parents love you; why don't *they* marry you?" *Ouch!* "Out of the abundance of the heart his mouth speaks" (Luke 6:45). With that simple and careless phrase, I knew that Michael was not thinking about buying me a ring anytime soon.

Prayer

Heavenly Father, please help us to guard our hearts with all diligence! You don't want your daughters to give their hearts away before it's time. Help us to wait on You, for we know that if we do things Your way, we will not be disappointed. And Lord, for every precious daughter whose heart is still breaking because she didn't guard her heart, I pray that You will pour out Your grace and Your healing balm of Gilead on her. Heal her heart, oh God. Defend her, protect her and build healthy levees around her heart once again—not that it would be hardened against future hurt but only more discerning and having an even greater capacity to love and be loved than before. For we know that "all things work together for good to those who love God, to those who are the called according to His purpose" [Rom. 8:28]. In Jesus' name, amen.

REFLECTIONS

1. Why is guarding your heart the most important thing you can do to protect yourself from heartache?
2. Have you ever given your heart away to the wrong person?
3. How do you get your heart back once you've given it away? Is that possible?

11

YOU ARE WORTH THE PRICE OF DINNER *AND* DESSERT

See what great love the Father has lavished on us,
that we should be called children of God!
1 JOHN 3:1, *NIV*

In today's world, who should pay on a date can sometimes be confusing. Stop right there! Ladies, there should be no confusion. The man pays. Yes, there are exceptions, but in general, especially when you are first going out, the man pays.

A few years ago, I was asked out by a college professor whom I assumed had a good-paying job, although the jalopy he drove and his sloppy appearance said otherwise. But it had been an embarrassingly long time since my last date, and I was determined to give this guy a chance. On our first date, he took me to a classy steakhouse, where we both enjoyed top-of-the-line steaks surrounded by an elegant atmosphere.

On our second date, we had pizza, and on our third date, we were at a cute little fish shack by the beach when this guy suddenly brought up the bill. "I think we should split the check," he said.

"Excuse me?" I said, more than a bit shocked. He went on to tell me about a platonic girlfriend whom he went out with occasionally and how he and her always split the check.

"Well, are you dating her?" I asked.

"No," he replied.

"Have you ever kissed her goodnight?" I asked.

"No."

I'm not sure where my words came from, but this is what I heard myself saying to him as I got up from my seat to go to the ladies' room: "I am worth the price of dinner *and* desert!" Ladies, the look on his face was priceless!

Not surprisingly, that was our last date. This man told me that I was extravagant and not a good steward of other people's money, namely his. He actually made me cry (not in front of him, but later)! I was so upset at being called extravagant simply because I had expected him to treat me like a lady that the next day at work, I asked one of my male co-anchors at the time, Lee Webb, what he thought about the situation. Lee affirmed what I felt deep in my heart: "When I was pursuing my wife, Donna, no expense was too great. I always paid and was happy to do so, not just for the ordinary but the extraordinary," he recalled. Lee also pointed out that God's love toward us is extravagant, not stingy. He cited 1 John 3:1: "What great love the Father has lavished on us" (*NIV*).

I love the word "lavish." It means "sumptuously rich and elaborate; to bestow something in generous or extravagant quantities upon; profuse, bounteous!"

Then Lee went on to say something that blew me away. Based on this Scripture, he said, "The pursuing man has the great opportunity to imitate God!" Wow. I was so blessed by Lee's words. A man has the privilege of being like God in his pursuit of a woman. Extravagant, lavish, generous, sumptuously rich! It still blows me away.

Listen to these great words from another male friend of mine. Shane writes,

If a guy is asking a girl out because he is attracted to her and has an interest in her long-term, paying for the date is an honor. It's an honor that she is willing to spend an evening with him. It's a small opportunity for him to make a good impression on her. Even in a situation where the woman is successful and the guy is not doing as well, paying for the date is a fundamental part of being a man. If he can't afford to date, he probably will not be able to afford a wife or a family. *And, just a little insight from my gender to yours: A man loves taking care of the woman he loves. He loves providing for her. It's at the core of being a man.* Maybe God set this system up so you girls would have a clue as to which guys have potential and which guys do not. I had a friend who had several daughters. When each of them turned 16, he took them out on their first date. Dad, of course, set a very high standard of etiquette. At the end of the night, he told each daughter, if you ever go out with a guy and he doesn't treat you the way I treated you tonight, don't go out with him again.

Another example: When my sister JeanAnne was dating her now husband Paul, not only did he always pay for dinner, but he bought her a brand-new car (while they were still dating) and later paid off her large student-loan debt soon after they were married! Now that's what I call extravagant.

When a man pays for dinner and a movie, it is a nice gesture, and it is appreciated, but expecting a man to pay simply for dinner—that's not extravagant, as the college professor tried to make me believe. Of course, if a guy flies you to Paris on his private jet and treats you to a romantic dinner on top of the Eiffel Tower, that's a different story. That would fall under the definition of extravagant. But seriously, when my sister's fiancé went the extra mile—buying her a car that she desperately needed and taking on her debt as his own—that's what I call lavish. That's what I call love.

"It made me feel like a princess," JeanAnne recalled. "And my prince had come to rescue me. He bought me a car because my hand-me-down car was so old, and the city is no place for an unreliable car. My safety was his number one concern, and that made me feel incredibly special, loved and secure. I knew he was showing me that he wanted to take care of me and proving that he wanted to be a good husband even before we walked down the aisle," JeanAnne remembered. "I had to kiss a lot of frogs before I met Paul, but I never gave up hope that one day God would send me my prince. Paul is more than I ever dreamed or imagined I would have in a husband," she said.

Fortunately with God, there is no confusion when it comes to His extravagant love for us:

> That Christ may dwell in your hearts through faith; that you, being rooted and grounded in love, may be able to comprehend with all the saints what is the width and length and depth and height—to know the love of Christ which passes knowledge; that you may be filled with all the fullness of God (Eph. 3:17-19).

I love the song, "Your Love is Extravagant," by Christian music artists Casting Crowns. It reminds us of how intimate God's love is and how he tries to capture our hearts. It also reminds us of how the love of Christ covers our sins and allows God to call us His friends. That's what I call extravagant.

Maybe it's not like this for all women, but I know that for me, if a man pays, it makes me feel more like a woman. I feel valued, safe, taken care of. It makes a statement. I recall that after my first date with the jalopy-driving professor at the nice steak house, he mentioned how expensive it was. Ouch. That's like saying, "I really didn't want to buy you that nice dinner."

And ladies, let's be real. If he can't afford to pay for your dinner, can he afford to buy you a ring? Can he afford a house for you both to live in? I'm not saying you should never pay for anything. When I am in a relationship, I like to occasionally buy breakfast or lunch or even cook for the guy—things my two sisters, who are now happily married, said they would never have done. But I feel that "official" date nights are his responsibility.

God wants you to know that you are worth the price of dinner *and* dessert—and so much more! You are worth someone being "extravagant," even lavish, over. After all, you are a daughter of the Most High King, a royal treasure, a beautiful masterpiece, a pearl of great price. You are a lady, and a true gentleman will recognize your value and act accordingly. Don't settle and don't forget to order dessert.

Prayer

Father, thank You for Your extravagant love that You lavish on Your children. Thank You for setting the example of how Your daughters should be treated. Help us to realize that if a man is not treating us the way You would treat us, than he is not "the one"! If he is cheap or stingy, he is not "the one"! Lord, thank You that we are worth not only the price of dinner and dessert but that You loved us so much that You gave your life for us! Help us never to underestimate our value—and always to remember that our true worth comes from the price You paid for us! In Jesus' name, amen.

REFLECTIONS

1. Have you ever dated someone who didn't want to pay for a meal or who asked you to pay half? How did that make you feel?
2. Why is God's extravagant love for us a good example of how a man should treat a woman he's pursuing?
3. What if a man can't afford to be extravagant financially? Are there other ways he can show that he's serious about pursuing a relationship with you?

12

THE RED HERRING

God never denies us our heart's desire except to give us something better.
ELISABETH ELLIOT

It was a beautiful Sunday evening, and I was driving back from what I thought had been a near-perfect weekend with a guy I had been dating only a few weeks. As I drove, I went over every detail of the romantic getaway: the dinner, the dress, the kiss. Suddenly and seemingly out of nowhere, a red car swerved in front of me and then quickly sped ahead, but not before I clearly saw its vanity license plate. It read: "REDHERNG." *Red herring.* It hit my spirit, and not in a good way.

God speaks to me in many ways, and over the years I've been surprised at how often He has spoken to me through vanity plates. As I mentioned once before, while on my way to hike Old Rag Mountain, I had glanced over and seen "GDNANGEL" on the license plate of the car driving next to me. It had made me smile, because I always feel close to God when I'm hiking and had received similar signs from Him during other hiking trips. Hours after seeing the plate, when I found myself hiking down the dark, scary mountain alone, I was comforted by that seemingly random experience. I knew that

God had allowed me to be in exactly the right spot on I-64 West to see that message.

Similarly, when I saw the "red herring" plate, I knew in my spirit that it was a sign. So when I got home, I Googled the meaning of the term.

A red herring is something that "misleads or detracts from the actual issue."[1] In an argument it is designed to divert an opponent's attention from the central issue. And in the literary world, get this: It is a false clue that will lead readers in the *wrong direction*. Yikes!

There are various theories on the origins of this phrase. One involves the practice of British fugitives from justice who were fleeing prison and being tracked by bloodhounds. In order to throw the dogs off their scent, the escapees would drag a red herring across their path to try to confuse the scent and divert the dogs. In murder mysteries a red herring is perfectly utilized when it interweaves itself into the story's events and takes the focus off the real perpetrator, leading the reader or the book's characters toward a false conclusion.[1]

In other words, red herrings are usually used to deliberately *mislead*.

The enemy of our souls loves to use red herrings to get us off track. He has been doing it since the beginning of time.

Genesis 3:1 says, "Now the serpent was more cunning than any beast of the field which the LORD God had made. And he said to the woman, 'Has God indeed said, 'You shall not eat of every tree of the garden'?'"

A red herring is anything that draws us away from God's best. In the Garden of Eden, Satan used an apple to entice Eve, convincing her that it was God's will for her to eat the forbidden fruit and to gain the knowledge of good and evil. Of course, that was not God's will, and history was changed forever by that one disobedient bite.

Satan tried a similar strategy with Jesus when the Lord was in the desert after a 40-day fast. The devil offered Jesus food, power and kingdoms if He would worship him, but Jesus was too smart to be deceived by Satan's red herrings and fought back with the Word of

God: "Jesus said to him, 'Away with you, Satan! For it is written, "You shall worship the LORD your God, and Him only you shall serve."' Then the devil left Him, and behold, angels came and ministered to Him" (Matt. 4:10-11).

The devil always wants us to settle for less than we deserve. He's the father of lies, confusion and deceit (see John 8:44). A red herring is designed to confuse us and to take our focus off the main goal. In a dating scenario, it will take our focus off God's perfect will or best match for us. Magicians use it to pull our attention away from what they are actually doing—so we will then *miss what really happened.*

The enemy wants us to miss God's best. He knows what we so desperately want and will often dangle something that looks very close to the real thing—also known as a counterfeit—right in front of us. What we see looks right, smells right, acts right—but somehow, deep in our spirit, we know that something is *not* right!

That night, after I saw the "red herring" vanity plate and researched its meaning, I had a sick feeling in the pit of my stomach. I knew that God was speaking to me. As I got down on my knees to pray, something definitely did not feel right to me about the guy I had started seeing. Oh, how I wish I could tell you that I heeded that feeling. But I did not. I continued to date this guy in the hopes that I was not being led in the wrong direction but was instead headed on the road to happiness, marriage and family.

Now that I look back, it's so clear that God was trying to open my eyes to the red herring that was distracting me so I could let him go and avoid the incredibly painful heartache that was just down the road. I pray that this will never happen to me again, and that it will never happen to you either.

I realize, of course, that God doesn't speak through every vanity plate we see on the road—thank goodness! That would be exhausting. But if you've been a Christian long enough, you know His voice, and you know when He's speaking to you, whether it's through a vanity plate or a cloud in the sky. God loves you and wants to protect you. Are we willing to trust Him when He speaks? That's the question. I know that God makes all things work together for good, even our wrong choices, but I don't think for a minute that He wanted me to get my heart broken. That's why He was trying to warn me: "Red herring! Don't believe it! It's a hoax; it's not real. You will be deceived! It's a trick! Run!"

Yes, sometimes it takes a lot of faith to heed God's warnings—but by all means, pay attention, study the signs, pray, and allow God to speak to you. And if at all possible, throw the red herrings back! God has the real deal for you.

Prayer

Lord, help us to heed Your warnings and not only to recognize a red herring but to be smart enough to throw it back. In Jesus' name, amen!

REFLECTIONS

1. Have you ever encountered a red herring—something meant to throw you off track from God's best for you?
2. Why is the enemy so obsessed with trying to get us to miss God's best?
3. How can we avoid falling for a red herring?

13

AVOID THE COUNTERFEIT

Deliver my soul, O LORD, from lying lips and from a deceitful tongue.
PSALM 120:2

Have you ever bought a gorgeous fake Prada bag or a pair of sleek faux Gucci sunglasses? My brothers, both of whom are lawyers, remind me that doing so may be illegal, so I'm definitely not encouraging you to break the law. But if you have ever bought any of these knock-off products, you probably really loved the deal you got at first but then, over time, you slowly began to notice the reason you were able to get that purse or that pair of sunglasses for such a cheap price: because *they were not the real thing.* They were made from substandard materials, so they broke or wore out much more quickly than the genuine article would have.

When it comes to the person you're dating or the person you hope to marry, would you settle for something close to the real thing? Or do you want the real deal? Of course you want the real thing. Just as that cheap pair of sunglasses snaps in two after only two weeks of wear or that strap breaks off your fake handbag as you walk into a restaurant, a fake partner in a relationship will leave you looking (and feeling) like a fool in the end. That's why—and I cannot stress this enough—it's so important to really get to know someone before you give them your heart.

What is a fake partner? It's simple. It's someone who is not real—someone who tries to act like the real thing but is instead a counterfeit. Like a red herring, the goal of the counterfeit is to deceive. We must be able to spot the counterfeit in the crowd even though he may look as real as those fake Coach sunglasses our best friend purchased for fifteen dollars.

Take a look at what "counterfeit" means: "made in imitation of something else with intent to deceive." I also like this definition: "something likely to be mistaken for something of higher value."

Because the counterfeit is by definition designed to confuse you, *your only hope of avoiding a trap is to listen to what God is saying in your spirit—to the still, small voice of God.*

> Jesus answered them, "My sheep hear My voice, and I know them, and they follow Me" (John 10:25,27).

> Your ears shall hear a word behind you, saying, "This is the way, walk in it," whenever you turn to the right hand or whenever you turn to the left (Isa. 30:21).

In a counterfeit relationship, the experiences you have may seem very real, but they are in reality insincere or feigned expressions of love—illusions that can deter you from finding and sharing real love.

I remember a relationship I had that seemed like "real love." I was convinced because my boyfriend was doing so many of the right things. But something extremely important was missing: certain words. He took me out to dinner, we went to church, we prayed together, we emailed and talked on the phone. And although he told me "I love you" and "I miss you" often, it was what he *wasn't* saying that should have been a red flag to me.

He wasn't talking about commitment in any real terms; he would instead confuse me by asking questions like, "If you were my wife, would you change your last name or keep it?" He would take me to look at new homes as if he was thinking of our future together. Remember, a counterfeit, like a red herring, is designed to cause confusion. And confusion is *not* from God: "For God is not the author of confusion but of peace, as in all the churches of the saints" (1 Cor. 14:33).

It's often said that a counterfeit comes right before the real thing when it comes to relationships. That may be true, but the more we know what real love looks and feels like, the more likely we will be able to spot the counterfeit before it's too late.

Again, I wish I could tell you that I heeded the Lord's warning after I saw the "red herring" vanity plate on the way back from that romantic weekend. But I did not. I continued dating the guy, and guess what? He eventually confessed to deceiving me. Counterfeits always deceive. It's their nature.

STEPS TO AVOID A COUNTERFEIT

1. *A man's intentions and feelings about you should be clear.* You shouldn't be forced to guess how he feels about you. The counterfeit guy I dated told me month after month, "God keeps telling me, 'One day a time.'" But if a guy doesn't know what his intentions are after several months of dating, he's "playing you, not planning with you," as author and comedian Steve Harvey says. Yes, I bought the "one day at a time" thing, and now I know what was happening—I was being played! Sometimes we have to learn things the hard way.

2. *Listen to God.* God will warn you. He loves you. He wants you to make good decisions, especially when it comes to your love life. I ignored numerous warning dreams from the Lord, because they didn't fit in with my fairy-tale plans. Don't ignore the little promptings, the red flags and the warning dreams. However God speaks

to you, pay close attention. We often need God's help to discern the real thing from the counterfeit.

3. *Make sure a man's words are consistent with his actions.* "I love you," "I miss you," "I need you" all sound wonderful, but they only ring true if a man's words match his actions. After months of "I love you's," if a guy's not popping the question to you, chances are that he's not really serious about you. Sincerity is proven by action. If you find a man consistent in his pursuit of you and who puts his words into action, you may have just found "the one."

Conversations Can Reveal a Counterfeit

After we broke up, I started to follow a popular pastor and author on Twitter. I had admired his wisdom teaching for years and am a big fan of his daily devotionals that come to my inbox each morning.

To my surprise, this pastor followed me on Twitter as well. I recognized a great opportunity to receive wisdom from him, so I tweeted him and told him that I was suffering from a broken heart and was having a hard time moving on. I asked him if he would pray for me. He immediately wrote back, saying that he would pray and asking me what had happened. So I told him, leaving out few details.

Once again, God used a man to help in my healing process. He had already used Dr. Pat Robertson to speak to my heart, and now He was using this pastor.

After I poured out my heart in an email, this is what he wrote back to me:

Precious Wendy,

I am in Zimbabwe, just coming in from a pastors' conference, teaching, etc. Your experiences remind me so much of my last serious relationship.

1. Your relentless returning shows that you invested your very, very best.
2. Confusion reveals the presence of a deceiver.
3. There are some missing conversations that this man will not have with you (whatever the reason).
4. You date from your heart. Few men truly treasure integrity, it appears.
5. Don't invest another hour, but do experiment/explore with conversations with others.
6. When the pain subsides, the wisdom it leaves is profound.

I have walked this kind of journey. Create some "oasis" for yourself along this road to divert your focus.

Keep me updated.

He was right. There was confusion (and confusion is not from God); there was deception (my boyfriend later admitted that he had deceived me); and there were conversations he would not have with me. More importantly, I had deceived myself and believed that I had to settle for less than God's best for me.

Just say no to the counterfeit. *You are a prize to be won.* Don't settle for less than God's best.

Charm Is Deceptive (Proverbs 31:30)

My friend Stacy Hord is a beautiful and accomplished author, speaker and single mother, who, unfortunately, has had some experience in dealing with the counterfeit. In her amazing story below, she shares how God opened her eyes to how the enemy can snare us with the illusive device known as charm.

I dated several men immediately following my divorce, but after two years of fruitless relationships, God gently encouraged me to take a time-out from dating. That time-out ended up lasting for six and a half years. When my sons graduated high school, I sought the Lord's release to return to the dating scene. I truly felt that six years of "good behavior" had prepared me to approach dating with much more knowledge. However, I was quite naive and quite wrong, for the enemy knew my weakness: impatience.

Within weeks, a man whom I was strongly attracted to contacted me. "Scott" was quite charming—so charming, in fact, that he literally wooed and charmed me right out of my senses. This man was in the ministry. He had an enormous amount of charisma and an ability to draw much attention to himself with his unique talents.

From the onset of our relationship, he showered me with gifts, surprises, songs, cards and creative dates. Every date with him was wildly exciting, and every womanly longing I had was filled by him. However, what started out looking so good ended up being not so good.

The emotional "highs" were exciting, but the relationship was primarily marked by strife and confusion, and although I continually sought the Lord for guidance, a heaviness that I could never understand or put my finger on was always in the recesses of my spirit. When I voiced my concerns to Scott, he countered aggressively, with an arsenal of reasons, that my doubts were out of God's will and that he was clearly the man for me. His reasoning always seemed to trump my uncertainties, and as the weeks wore on and he pushed for marriage, my confusion increased.

About two months into the relationship, extreme jealousy and possessiveness from Scott began to emerge. Simple conversations quickly spiraled into accusations that I was cheating and hiding things from him, leaving me bewildered. Any window of time during which he couldn't reach me I had to account for, and any conversations I had with men, including the men I worked with and were in ministry with, were scrutinized. Over each event I was questioned, accused, shamed and forbidden to talk to men. The relationship slowly became a godless pit, and I found myself crying out to God to get me out of it.

The straw that broke the camel's back finally came when I was on a ministry trip. Scott's constant phone calls, questioning and accusations distracted and angered me so much that I could not focus on the purpose of the mission. My eyes were opened, and I realized that if I could not travel and minister without the endless insecurities and interference of this man, I would not be able to do God's work. I finally found the strength to break off the relationship.

Within days of the breakup, several of my relatives, friends and ministry partners received emails and messages from Scott asking them to help me because I had "let Satan get a hold" of me and was "in sin." He sent me a barrage of messages calling me a liar, a sinner and demonic. Then, in a strange twist of manipulation, he threatened that if I did not get back together with him, he would ruin my ministry. I was left in a stupor. I had been duped.

THE SHINY WRAPPER

So I sought God for the answers. How had something that had looked so good up front and even godly on the exterior become so devastating? That's when God gave me the "shiny wrapper" wisdom.

You see, God does not work in the ways of earthly wisdom. His ways are humbling to us, and they almost always involve painful waiting. Satan's ways are the opposite. He satisfies our flesh with the easy, the fast, the appealing and the sensual, and these are all wrapped up in a shiny wrapper that looks like a gift from above. The world loves this. The bait is clever and charming and always hooks us, because our natural tendencies always lean toward what makes us feel good.

All women love attention, wonderfully planned dates, adoration, gifts and flowers. Isn't extravagant romance, the kind we see in the movies, the most important thing? I certainly thought it was, and it has its place for sure, but it can also be a front to beguile and distract us from what is truly behind the mask of the romancer.

This deception, a common ploy of Satan to track and snare us, is commonly called the art of misdirection—an elusive tactic used in many settings such as warfare, hunting, theater and magic. It is essentially the same thing we do when we have only one fudge bar left in the freezer and we want to hide it from the rest of the family, so we place it behind something we know will be a great cover: the broccoli. The fudge bar is there, but it is well hidden. God showed me that this is how Satan works—he hides behind what looks innocent and good. Just because we see something that looks good up front doesn't mean that it is truly good—Satan's facade could very well be at work.

By the time Scott's true ways surfaced, I was emotionally caught in our relationship like a rabbit in a trap. I wanted to leave, but I couldn't, even though the abuses in the relationship intensified. The gratification that had hooked me soon engulfed me. Scott's (counterfeit) love had been intoxicating and addictive but slowly became suffocating and demanding. The demands of the relationship became so strong that they stole my joy, and all I had left was an addiction—a perfect picture of how Satan works.

Satan works from the beginning to the end, luring us from the beginning with appealing, quick satisfaction that will slowly and ultimately drag us down to a deathly end. Conversely, God works from the end to the beginning by first placing the end in our heart: His promise. Then He begins

the slow and painful process of allowing our flesh to die so
that the dream can finally live. Our promise will come by His
power and *only* by His power.

> But God chose the foolish things of the world to shame
> the wise; God chose the weak things of the world to
> shame the strong. God chose the lowly things of this
> world and the despised things—and the things that are
> not—to nullify the things that are, so that no one may
> boast before him (1 Cor. 1:27-29, *NIV*).

God doesn't send things to us in a shiny, pretty wrapper—
the enemy does. The devil does this to tempt us and lure us,
drawing us by the lust of our flesh. God, on the other hand,
works *against* our flesh, bringing things about through humble
and unseemly means. That is why Jesus was born in a humble
stable instead of a magnificent mansion. God doesn't want us
to fall for the "shiny wrapper" bit. He wants to *birth* a relationship for us from humble means, from something that seems
impossible through our own means but is entirely possible
through God's power.

Eighteenth-century preacher William Plumer said, "We often tremble to see God pursuing a course which to our short
sight, seems quite contrary to the end to be gained. This is for
two purposes. The first is to humble us and thus prepare us
for the reception of his great blessings. The other is to prove
that besides him there is no savior."

Sweet sister, God has wrapped up your promise not with
a shiny wrapper but with a cross. All your gifts from God,
including marriage, must pass through the cross first. Why?
Because the cross purifies, humbles and removes all our selfish motives and pride. If Satan could have seen what was on
the other side of the cross, he would have done everything he
could have to keep Jesus from going to it. But Satan cannot

see beyond the cross, so God has put one in front of His promise to you so that Satan cannot see God's plans for your life. What comes by way of the cross is lasting, fulfilling, anointed and blessed. You don't want a promise that hasn't been through the fire of the cross.

THE WAY OF THE CROSS

What is the cross? It involves waiting, pain and humility. If you have been painfully waiting and trusting God, then you are going to receive your promise in an uncommon but miraculous way. This is the way that the great patriarchs of the Bible received their promises, and it is the way we receive ours today. No doubt this way is painful and sometimes humiliating. It is not easy to watch our girlfriends find great guys, marry and have families while we patiently wait for God. We are tempted to get angry at God for His delays, and to want to go our own way to get a man now. But as my story has shown, that way only provides heartache in the end.

You must be asking at this point, "How then does it feel when the *right* guy comes along?" I can't answer that for every situation, but the Bible does provide us with an example of how it feels to be in the presence of the true Spirit of God. In the book of Luke, chapter 24, Jesus had just risen from the grave, but many of His disciples were not aware of this fact yet. Two of His disciples were walking along a road when a man came up behind them and began to walk with them. They did not realize that this was Jesus in His new body. As they spoke with Him, they were drawn to this strange man in the deepest of ways. Verses 30-32 give us insight into how Jesus revealed Himself to them:

> When he was at the table with them, he took bread, gave thanks, broke it and began to give it to them. Then their eyes were opened and they recognized

him, and he disappeared from their sight. They asked
each other, "Were not our hearts burning within us
while he talked with us on the road and opened the
Scriptures to us?" (Luke 24:30-32, *NIV*).

The breaking of bread typifies Christian fellowship.
The man God has for you will feel comfortable serving next
to you with your Christian friends and family. He will not try
in any way to separate you from God's people, and a spirit of
thanks will be in your heart for this man's love for the Body
of Christ.

But the most telling event in the scenario with these disciples is how the hearts of the two men burned within them
when Jesus was with them. When He spoke, the gifts in them
were stirred, and their love for God was kindled, and the Scriptures were the foundation of their relationship with Him. This
is exactly how God wants things to be when you are in the presence of the man He has for you. He wants your spiritual gifts to
be stirred, your desires for God warmed and the Bible to be the
foundation for your decisions together. No *man* can warm your
heart like that—only God can. You will be drawn to the Spirit
of Jesus in the right man. Is that worth waiting for? I think so.

THE LONGER THE WAIT, THE BIGGER THE BLESSING

Sweet sister, don't let the length of waiting be a stumbling
block to you. It's a well-known fact in the kingdom of God
that the longer the wait, the bigger the blessing. This period
of waiting is an important part of the process that God will
not neglect, because He cares for our futures too much. Many
relationships start on a false premise, but God wants to guard
us against that by providing us His own security system. Waiting is part of that system.

At this writing, I have been waiting ten years, and I will say
that although the journey has been hard at times, it has been

sweet and fruitful. God has finally weaned me from the idealizations that led me right into the traps of the enemy. I am content, free and truly enjoying my single years. I thought my thirst was for a man, but I realize now that my thirst was for Jesus, and He has totally quenched my desires. Don't fall for the shiny wrapper. Fall for Jesus, and see what wonderful things He will bring your way.

Prayer

Dear heavenly Father, thank You for protecting Stacy and all of us from the counterfeits. Open our eyes and help us to always discern the counterfeit from the real thing. Lord, help us to heed Your warnings and Your still small voice so we won't end up with heartache and regrets. Lord, I pray that there will be no more counterfeits in my life or in the lives of any of my sisters. No more red herrings! Lord, thank You that You have only the best for me and for all of Your daughters. Help us to wait on Your best and nothing less and to recognize it when it comes. In Jesus' name, amen.

REFLECTIONS

1. Have you ever dated a counterfeit?
2. How can we recognize a counterfeit relationship from the real thing?
3. How does asking the right questions help uncover a counterfeit?

14

THE DANGERS OF RECREATIONAL KISSING

Can a man take fire to his bosom, and his clothes not be burned?
Can one walk on hot coals, and his feet not be seared?
PROVERBS 6:27-28

I remember it as if it were yesterday—the voice of the Holy Spirit saying, *Wendy, you're feeling vulnerable because you're giving yourself away.* Giving myself away? During my relationship with Michael, we weren't having sex; we were only kissing, as we believed strongly in saving sex for marriage. So how could just kissing be giving myself away?

But the Holy Spirit was right. I *was* feeling vulnerable. I didn't know where Michael and I stood. Was he in love with me or just attracted to me physically? Was he thinking about us long term? Planning a future for us? He hadn't exactly said so, but he did ask me to go look at houses with him, and he did ask to look at my financials and to help me with a budget. Aren't those pre-husband types of things? Plus, he had invited me to spend Thanksgiving and

Christmas with his family. So why was I feeling so vulnerable, so emotionally out on a limb?

Suddenly I remembered something I had written in my journal some months before.

JOURNAL ENTRY
JULY 11, 2011

Father, something in me is warning me to "guard my heart" and not give away my kisses so easily. Help me, Lord! Fight for me and give me strength—Your strength!

Hmmm . . . the Holy Spirit had known something I had not. He had seen a heartache on the horizon and had wanted to protect me. But stubborn-headed as I was, I ignored His warnings to slow down, to back up, to take a break from all the lip-locking and find out what was really in Michael's heart concerning me. One thing was for sure: With every kiss I was sinking deeper into the quagmire of love—or the fantasy of love that I had willingly conjured up in my head.

Kissing—hello!—is much more intimate than we might realize. It's lips on lips, breath on breath. And French kissing—well, that's a whole different story. It's pretty much having sex with your clothes on. You know it's true. And that's why I was feeling so vulnerable. This kind of intimacy felt like sex to me, and emotionally speaking, it may as well have been.

Science proves what I'm saying. Kissing releases feel-good chemicals in the brain, such as endorphins and dopamine. Dopamine is largely responsible for the feelings of pleasure we experience when we kiss. But endorphins, which are peptides, can also lead to feelings of euphoria. It's no wonder some people say that passionate kissing is like a drug. Kissing is highly addictive and keeps us coming back for more. There should be a warning label somewhere:

No Recreational Kissing Allowed!
May lead you to think you're falling in love with
someone just because he's a good kisser but who is
in reality totally wrong for you!

Funny thing was, before I met Michael, I had a lot of platonic male friends whom I enjoyed hanging out with but nobody I could imagine myself kissing or being romantic with. One night, after yet another platonic date, I prayed earnestly, "Lord, please, when are you going to send me someone I want to kiss?" Be careful what you pray for. You may just get it.

So am I advocating no kissing until you're married? Maybe . . . I'm not saying it would be easy but it might be a good idea for those of us who fall in love with the first kiss.

Today, while writing this chapter, I happened to turn on the television, and a Christian movie called *Pamela's Prayer* was on. It's about a 16-year-old Christian girl who desperately wanted to start dating the way all her friends were, but her protective father did not want her to yet. She told him that he was old fashioned and making her life miserable, and she disobeyed him and went out with a boy who then told everyone he had kissed her when she had actually refused his kiss. She was devastated and promised never to lie to her father again.

Her dad forgave her and said to her, "Pamela, on your wedding night, when you're lying there next to your husband, don't you want to be able to tell him that you never kissed another boy but saved all your love for him? And don't you want someone who didn't fool around and kiss a lot of other girls but saved all his kisses and love for you?"

"Yes, Dad, that's what I want," she said. "I want a guy who has saved all his love for me."

As I watched this touching scene, I burst into tears! It was such a powerful moment between a father, who wanted nothing but the best for his daughter, and a young girl, who was having a hard time understanding why she had to wait. It was a perfect picture of God's heart for His children and how He yearns for His daughters and sons to know and experience purity before marriage—not to keep them from pleasure but to keep them from pain.

In the movie Pamela wondered if it was even possible to meet a boy who had never kissed another girl but was waiting, as she was, to have their first kiss on their wedding day. Not long after she thought about that, a handsome young high-school senior started working for her dad, and after a few years, this young man discovered that he and Pamela were likeminded on the topic of sexual purity before marriage. He proposed to her at Christmas, and their first kiss was on their wedding day.

Maybe there's a reason that the preacher always says, "*Now* you may kiss your bride."

Does a Kiss Really Tell?

"How in the world can you tell if you want to marry somebody if you've never kissed them?" Elisabeth Elliot, in her classic book *Passion and Purity*, says that this was a question she often received from students. Her reply: "But how in the world can you tell you want to marry somebody just because you've kissed them?" Intimacy is not necessary, Elliot argues, in order for us to know if we want to marry someone.

She goes on to talk about how Isaac had no "practice run" with Rebekah before they married. His marriage was, in fact, arranged:

> When Abraham sent his servant to find a wife for Isaac, there was no question of any tryouts by means of intimacy. The servant, the third party, had to look her over and assess her worth and suitability. He went to the logical place—the spring outside the city, where the women would come. He prayed silently, watching all the time. He had specifically asked God to give him a sign: The girl whom he asked for a drink would not only give him one, but would also water

his camels. The servant continued "watching quietly to see whether or not the Lord had made his journey successful."[1]

In another example, Elliot reminds us that Ruth did not kiss Boaz before their wedding vows; instead, she followed Naomi's instructions in her courtship with Boaz:

> Then Naomi her mother-in-law said to her, "My daughter, shall I not seek security for you, that it may be well with you? Now Boaz, whose young women you were with, is he not our relative? In fact, he is winnowing barley tonight at the threshing floor. Therefore wash yourself and anoint yourself, put on your best garment and go down to the threshing floor; but do not make yourself known to the man until he has finished eating and drinking. Then it shall be, when he lies down, that you shall notice the place where he lies; and you shall go in, uncover his feet, and lie down; and he will tell you what you should do." And she said to her, "All that you say to me I will do" (Ruth 3:1-5).

Elliot continues, "I had put [Jim Elliot] down as the sort of man I hoped to marry. Kissing and holding hands would have added nothing to this conviction (anybody can kiss and hold hands). On the contrary, in fact, it would have subtracted something very important."[2]

Elliot makes the case that observing a person's character qualities and spending time together with him as friends is basis enough to know if you could marry him—not because you've felt the euphoria from his kiss. I would tend to agree.

A Potentially Unmanageable Force

In the telling of her courtship, Elliot writes about how she and Jim tried to "live honestly before God" and keep each other at arm's length before marriage, which she admits was much easier said than done. But by God's grace, they managed to do it.

> We recognized that we were strongly drawn toward each other. There were "butterflies" when we were near. Those perfectly human, perfectly natural appetites were being whetted with every slightest touch, and the idea of a good long scrunch [kiss] or even a single short kiss seemed like heaven itself.
>
> Honesty required us to admit that we could not be sure precisely where the "line" *should* be drawn, and it was a potentially unmanageable force we were dealing with. Chastity meant for us not taking lightly any least act or thought that was not appropriate to the kind of commitment we had to God."[3]

Elisabeth and Jim Elliot ended up having their first kiss when he finally proposed marriage in the jungles of Quito, Ecuador, and put a ring on her finger five long years after they first met.

And their honeymoon, in the words of Elisabeth, "was unspeakably worth the wait."[4]

In today's modern world people are astonished when someone takes a stand for purity. "But why wait?" they argue. "Everybody lives together and has sex." If we take a stand for purity, we must be ready to be thought of as weird by the majority around us. But I'd rather be thought of as weird or even prudish than to live with regrets, wouldn't you?

> This is the will of God, that you should be holy; you must abstain from fornication; each one of you must learn to gain mastery over his body, to hallow and honour it, not giving way to lust like the pagans who are ignorant of God; and no man must do his brother wrong in this matter, or invade his rights, because as we told you before with all emphasis, the Lord punishes all such offences. For God called us to holiness, not to impurity. Anyone therefore who flouts these

rules is flouting, not man, but God who bestows upon you his Holy Spirit (1 Thess. 4:3-8, *NEB*).

I have a friend whom I admire greatly who did not kiss her husband until they were engaged. She often says, "It wasn't how far we could go but how much we could save that was important. I remember the first time he held my hand. It was so precious to me. The innocence of it moved my heart."

As the line from the movie *The Count of Monte Cristo* said, "God is in everything—even in a kiss." God may not be in *every* kiss, but he was definitely in the kiss between Mercedes and the Count of Monte Cristo in the movie named for the count. This story, by the way, is a must-see for romance lovers.

I know too that God was definitely in the kisses between Solomon and his bride, because the Bible says so:

Let him kiss me with the kisses of his mouth—for your love is better than wine. Because of the fragrance of your good ointments, your name is ointment poured forth; therefore the virgins love you. Draw me away! (Song of Sol. 1:2-4).

One thing that I have learned the hard way is that kissing is truly special and should not be something you do casually with just anybody. It's too dangerous a force! "Don't give your kisses away for free," the Holy Spirit warned me.

Our kisses are valuable. They are worth so much more than we realize, because with every kiss, we give a little bit of our heart and of ourselves away. Save your kisses; store them up for that special person whom God has handpicked for you. If you've been impatient or made mistakes, then repent, ask God to forgive you, and forgive yourself. With Jesus, there's always a fresh start. Then set yourself to wait for God's timing.

I don't know about you, but I want to be able to say, as Elisabeth Elliot did, that "it was unspeakably worth the wait."

Prayer

Lord, help us to remember that it's not how much we can give away now but how much we can save that counts. Even a kiss can be wrong if it's given to the wrong person or given in the wrong timing. Lord, give us wisdom and strength to wait for the one who will not only be worth kissing but who will value our kisses as special treasures for a lifetime. In Jesus' name, amen.

REFLECTIONS

1. When is the proper time for a first kiss?
2. Why can passionate kissing become a problem in a developing relationship?
3. What is the best-case scenario for kissing in a relationship?

15

PURITY IS SEXY

Every time you give a part of yourself away to the wrong person,
it takes away the wonder.

ANONYMOUS

It was only our second date, and since Michael was from out of town, we were trying to make it last. With no restaurants open at eleven at night, we went to my house and sat on my red leather couch in front of the cozy fireplace (not too smart if you are trying to avoid temptation). But our relationship was so new, and I wasn't even sure if we were compatible yet, so I rationalized that it would be okay.

As we sat and talked and got to know each other, Michael suddenly said, "I love your innocence." I wasn't sure, however, if that was a compliment. I was wearing a red dress with black stiletto heels that I could hardly walk in, and I was hoping to be seen as a sophisticated and successful woman who could walk in six-inch heels, not an innocent little girl. Although one of the definitions of "innocence" is "lack of worldly experience or sophistication," it has other meanings that are quite attractive: "freedom from guilt or sin through being unacquainted with evil: blamelessness" and "chastity."[1] Those are definitely good things.

Looking back now, I think Michael meant it as a compliment. Hopefully, what he was referring to was my heart and my desire to

please the Lord in all things, including dating. As he and I continued
to see more and more of each other, it became increasingly difficult
for us to stay within safe boundaries. It was around that time that
I heard the Holy Spirit say to me, "Practice purity." The Holy Spirit
wanted me to practice being pure. It was extremely valuable advice—
actually a command from the Lord designed to protect Michael and
me from going too far too fast.

But since we weren't having sex, what did it mean to be pure?
Purity is defined as "the condition or quality of being pure; freedom
from anything that debases, contaminates, pollutes, etc.," "ceremo-
nial or ritual cleanness," "freedom from guilt or evil; innocence," and
as "physical chastity; virginity."[2]

The Bible has much to say about sexual purity:

Flee sexual immorality. Every sin that a man does is outside the body, but he who commits sexual immorality sins
against his own body (1 Cor. 6:18).

Marriage should be honored by all, and the marriage bed
kept pure, for God will judge the adulterer and all the sexually immoral (Heb. 13:4, *NIV*).

It is God's will that you should be sanctified: that you should
avoid sexual immorality; that each of you should learn to
control your own body in a way that is holy and honorable,
not in passionate lust like the pagans, who do not know God
(1 Thess. 4:3-5, *NIV*).

I say to you that whoever looks at a woman to lust for
her has already committed adultery with her in his heart
(Matt. 5:28).

No temptation has overtaken you except such as is common
to man; but God is faithful, who will not allow you to be

tempted beyond what you are able, but with the temptation will also make the way of escape, that you may be able to bear it (1 Cor. 10:13).

Apparently, this was an area that the Lord knew people would struggle with, because there are dozens more Scriptures that deal with the issue of moral and sexual purity. (Here are a few that you may want to look up and study on your own Psalm 119:37; Romans 6:11-14; Galatians 5:19-21; Colossians 3:5 and James 1:13-14.)

Innocence and purity are not qualities that the world seems to prize much these days. Turn on the television, even during prime time—or especially during prime time—and it's one sexual innuendo after another. Good luck finding a television actor who portrays a person of high moral character. You'll have to watch *The Waltons* or *Little House on the Prairie* to find those kinds of characters.

Although innocence is certainly underrated and rare these days, it is definitely something we want in a mate. We might say that innocence increases a person's value. It did for the Proverbs 31 woman: "Who can find a virtuous [morally excellent] woman? For her price [worth] is far above rubies" (Prov. 31:10, *KJV*).

The idea of staying pure before marriage is so bizarre and so foreign to some in the media that celebrities such as NFL football player Tim Tebow and American track and field Olympian Lolo Jones, who have announced that they're waiting to have sex until they're married, are routinely made fun of. Tebow is often referred to as a Jesus freak and is as famous for his commitment to virginity as he is for his skills as a quarterback. One liberal website asked, "Do you think Tebow's prudishness is a waste or totally wonderful?" The fact that they even posed the question leads me to believe that while they're busy making fun of the famous virgins for their commitment to save sex until marriage, they secretly admire them for their strength of conviction and their strong biblical values.

Yes, purity is sexy. What could be sexier then saving yourself for your beloved until your wedding night? I can't think of a better wedding gift to give, can you? And what peace you and your spouse will both have in knowing you did things God's way. There will be none of the guilt that comes from opening a gift before Christmas, so to speak. And I know that if I marry a man who shows restraint before marriage, I will be assured of his faithfulness after marriage too.

Think about this: Why do so many honeymoon resorts have to offer a wide range of extracurricular activities, including water aerobics, parasailing, beach volleyball, jet-skiing, snorkeling, etc.? It's probably because most of the newlyweds visiting those resorts have already lived together or had sex dozens of times, so they need other activities to keep them entertained. Now I've snorkeled, sailed, hiked and jet-skied all over the world, and those are fun things to do, but I'm going to be honest with you—those kinds of activities are not what my honeymoon is going to be about! Okay, so there may be some time for hiking—I can't resist a great hike. And perhaps some lounging poolside with fruity drinks. But you get my point!

In the meantime, I'm praying that my future husband will be sexually pure. Sure, he may have made some mistakes in the past, but hopefully he is now living a life of sexual purity. And in an age in which Internet pornography use is common even among church-goers, I'm especially praying that my future husband is guarding his eyes.

Job prayed over his eyes that he would not lust after women: "I have made a covenant with my eyes; why then should I look upon a young woman?" (Job 31:1).

Guarding our eyes is a full-time job in today's society. We see scantily clad women everywhere, from billboards to movies to Internet ads to the underwear catalogs that fill our mailboxes on a weekly basis. It takes a strong man to say, "No, I won't allow myself to look at those images and to lust in my heart."

In the movie *Fireproof*, which is about a couple's struggle to keep their marriage alive, the husband, Caleb (played by actor Kirk Cameron), realizes that he has a problem with Internet pornography and that his habit is threatening his marriage. He takes his computer outside and smashes it with a hammer while the neighbors look on, bewildered. Sometimes it takes extreme action to get free.

A guy friend of mine confessed that he was struggling in this area, and he had a friend of his who knew a lot about computers and could block all those sites so he couldn't access them. He was a godly man who knew that he needed help in this area. Today he's walking in sexual purity and waiting for God to send him the right woman. That woman will be blessed because of the integrity my friend is showing now as a single man.

I'm praying for a man who will do whatever it takes to guard his eyes. I want him to have eyes only for me—and not to be haunted by airbrushed images of perfect bodies he's seen online. Too many women have been heartbroken by men with the wandering-eye syndrome.

But let's be real. It's not only men who need to discipline their eyes—we women do too.

Of course, there's a difference between lusting after someone of the opposite sex while having impure thoughts about them and simply admiring God's creation. I recently saw the new Superman movie, *Man of Steel*, starring British actor Henry Cavill as Superman. I was privileged to interview Cavill at the Warner Brothers Studios in Los Angeles two weeks before the film debuted. Cavill is a charming and handsome man with an amazing work ethic and an incredible physique. After all, he is the Man of Steel. Cavill told me that he had endured grueling workouts to get in shape for his role—and it certainly paid off. I'm sure that there are thousands of women like myself across the globe who admire this man for his dedication to his career and for his level of fitness. But that's where it must end for me and for the thousands of women like me, and the same goes for all those men who notice beautiful women on the street, on a magazine or in a movie.

It sometimes takes effort to keep our mind and our heart pure and not to allow admiration or appreciation of God's handiwork to turn into something ugly and lustful. But the Bible is clear when it comes to sexual temptation: Flee! Run for your life! "Run from sexual sin! No other sin so clearly affects the body as this one does. For sexual immorality is a sin against your own body" (1 Cor. 6:18, *NLT*)

When we are faced with temptation, maybe it would help if we asked ourselves, *Would God approve of these thoughts and feelings I'm having?* When in doubt, pray for God's help with this prayer:

> *Search me, O God, and know my heart; try me, and know my anxious thoughts; and see if there is any wicked or wrong way in me, and lead me in the way everlasting [see Ps. 139:23-24]. Help me to appreciate beauty without falling into a trap of sin and lust. Help me to keep my eyes on the prize! In Jesus' name, amen.*

Guarding Your Mind—Just Say No to Fantasizing

My friend Stacy Hord has this warning about fantasizing in her terrific book *A New Vision for Dating*:

> You must learn to control your thought life. You cannot allow yourself to fantasize about the opposite sex for even a second. The second you allow fantasy to take over, you have changed from the driver's seat to the back seat, and your mind is a maniacal driver. If you are attracted to your boss and are tempted to fantasize about him, *don't.* Not your boss, or your professor, or your preacher, or your neighbor, or another parent on your child's soccer team, or your best friend's spouse. Not even Hollywood actors, or athletes or political figures. *No one.* Do not fantasize about *anyone.* Not even someone you just started dating. Fantasizing will take you into zones that can ruin a relationship. It may seem harmless in the beginning, but it is powerful and feeds desires inside of you that know no boundaries.[3]

There Is Forgiveness

The good news is that even if you or your future spouse have done things with the opposite sex that you regret, Jesus says, "I make all things new" (Rev. 21:5). Can Jesus make you a virgin again? No, but He can make you pure again. When we believe in Him and receive His free gift of salvation, He takes our sins upon Himself: "As far as the east is from the west, so far has He removed our transgressions [sins] from us" (Ps. 103:12).

He can even wash you until you are as white as snow:

> "Come now, and let us reason together," says the LORD, "though your sins are like scarlet, they shall be as white as snow; though they are red like crimson, they shall be as wool" (Isa. 1:18).

When you have been forgiven and are walking again in sexual purity, you can feel like a "born-again virgin."

Benefits of Staying Pure

The benefits of staying pure outweigh the temporary thrills of sexual sin by about a trillion light years. Bestselling author Joshua Harris, in his outstanding book *Boy Meets Girl*, highlights this: "Romantic passion awakened without commitment can lead to sin and regret."[4]

Truer words have never been spoken. I'm here to tell you that even though Michael and I didn't have sex, I regret all the kissing. Yes, at the time it felt exhilarating and fun, but I now regret that it led me to give my heart to a man who did not make a commitment to me—although he did a really good job of pretending that he was committed to me. He even once told me, "You are essentially my spouse." It certainly gave me the impression that he was thinking of me in those terms. I took little phrases like that and turned them into something they weren't: a commitment! And with every make-out session, I convinced myself that we were that much closer to walking down the aisle.

Trust me, you don't have to give everything away to feel vulnerable or even to feel violated—even if you were a willing participant, as I was. But most people, including a lot of Christians, say, "Oh, kissing is innocent. You have to kiss to know if you're compatible, to see if you have chemistry. What if he's a bad kisser?"

Would someone please tell that to my heart? Perhaps that's why Solomon urges the daughters of Jerusalem to not "awaken love" until the proper time: "I charge you, O daughters of Jerusalem, by the gazelles or by the does of the field, do not stir up nor awaken love until it pleases" (Song of Sol. 2:7).

Joshua Harris shares a few principles that helped him and his future wife Shannon during their courtship and engagement. The first is this:

> *During courtship, guarding each other's purity and refraining from sexual intimacy are the acts of lovemaking.* A Christian man and woman in love have to . . . renew their thinking so that they both see that not violating their future marriage bed is a true expression of love.[5]

Satan Wants to Steal the Value of Kissing and Sex

Anything that God has declared good—and God has declared sex to be very good within the bounds of marriage—Satan wants to corrupt, pervert and destroy.

Satan is the father of lies. His mission is to steal, kill and destroy (see John 10:10). He wants to destroy not only your sex life but everything concerning your life, especially if you are a child of God. His strategy is as old as the Garden of Eden. He tries to make you think that God is holding out on you, that you're deprived of the good stuff, that you're missing out on all the fun. In the garden Satan whispered to Eve concerning the tree of the knowledge of good and evil, "Has God indeed said, 'You shall not eat of every tree of the garden'?" (Gen. 3:1).

Eve replied, "We may eat the fruit of the trees of the garden; but of the fruit of the tree which is in the midst of the garden, God has said, 'You shall not eat it, nor shall you touch it, lest you die'" (3:2-3). Eve's answer seemed pretty strong, but the serpent, who the Bible says was more cunning that any of the beasts of the field, was not ready to give up. Perhaps Eve was beginning to look longingly at the tree and its beautiful fruit that she had never tasted and maybe even to question God's goodness in keeping that fruit from her and Adam. Satan, seeing perhaps that she was taking the bait, went in for the kill: "You will not surely die. For God knows that in the day you eat of it your eyes will be opened, and you will be like God, knowing good and evil" (3:4-5).

The serpent's devious lie led to Eve's wrong thinking, which led to her wrong action. "Then the eyes of both of them were opened and they knew that they were naked" (3:7). Adam and Eve's newly gained awareness brought them not the promised knowledge of good and evil, but embarrassment and shame over their nakedness.

Adam and Eve's disobedience also led to what's known as the fall of humankind. They went from walking and talking with God in the garden in the cool of the evening, to being cast out of the garden and having to toil and labor over the land to produce their food. "In the sweat of your face you shall eat bread" (3:19).

What's so sad is that they could still see the garden where they used to be so happy, carefree and innocent, but it was now heavily guarded by angels and a flaming sword, "which turned every way, to guard the way to the tree of life" (3:24). There was no going back.

Fortunately for humanity, God sent His beloved Son, Jesus, to Earth to die for us, that whoever believes in Him will not perish but have everlasting life (see John 3:16). Jesus made a way for us to have fellowship again with the Father. He said, "I am the way, the truth, and the life; no one comes to the Father except through Me" (14:6). So that's the good news. We can be forgiven for our sins and our shortcomings in the area of sexual purity.

The bad news is Satan is still lurking around. He may be clever, but he's still using the same old tricks he used back in the garden. When it comes to sex, he'll try to entice us with questions such as, *"Did God really say sex before marriage is a sin?"* or *"You're two people in love—how could it be wrong?"* or, *"It's okay to do everything except . . ."*

Joshua Harris writes, "Lust would like us to believe that it can make us happy. If we just give it what it wants, it will stop pestering us and be satisfied. Don't buy it. *Lust is never satisfied. . . . Lust hijacks sex. It wants to train your desires to delight in the thrill of the forbidden so that you lose your godly appetite for what is good.*"[6]

My friend Stacy Hord says the same thing in another way: "Sex within a marriage is wonderful and totally fulfilling, but sex before marriage is a giant that will take you captive, keeping you from the real pleasure God wants to show you with His blessing."[7]

Satan, however, knows how great sex is within the bounds of a loving committed marriage, and he's committed to trying to rob you of that joy by getting you to take a bite of the "fruit" before it's time.

Prayer

Heavenly Father, help us to practice purity. Help us to guard not only our hearts but our eyes and our minds. Give us Your view of sexuality, and help us to understand that sex is a gift only to be opened with the special person You have for us within the safety and the covenant of marriage. Lord, it's not easy waiting, but You wouldn't call us to do something that we can't do. And Lord, for those of us who have fallen short in this area, thank You for Your wonderful forgiveness, for washing us clean and for making us new again. Give us strength, Lord, so that we can enjoy the blessings that come from being sexually pure. In Jesus' name, amen.

REFLECTIONS

1. What does the Bible say about the importance of sexual purity before marriage?
2. Can purity be sexy?
3. Why is waiting until marriage for sex the best-case scenario?

16

DON'T LOOK BACK

Do not remember the former things, nor consider the things of old.
Behold, I will do a new thing, now it shall spring forth; shall you not know
it? I will even make a road in the wilderness and rivers in the desert.
ISAIAH 43:18-19

My friend Charlene likes to say, "Girl, there's nothing in the rearview mirror for you."

She's right. Think how hard it would be to drive toward your future destination if your eyes were constantly on the rearview mirror. First of all, you're asking for an accident, and second, it's not likely you're going to get anywhere.

But why is it that those lousy crumbs—those few good memories you shared with someone, the few times he really did seem crazy about you—can sometimes feel so tantalizing, as if there's an unseen magnet trying to pull you to go back to Crumbsville? I'll tell you why: When all we've ever known is crumbs, when all we've ever experienced is crumbs, we'll crave the crumbs!

A crumb is defined as "a small particle of bread, cake, etc. that has broken off; a small portion of anything; fragment; bit." But guess what? God doesn't want us to settle for crumbs! In fact, He says that if we won't settle, He will give us His best. God says to us, "I will do exceedingly, abundantly greater things than you can think, dream or imagine!" (see Eph 3:20). God will do *more* for us than we ask!

Case in Point

As I mentioned earlier in the book, after several months of no communication, Michael sent me an email: "I miss you. Can I come and see you this weekend?" Although I had ignored his previous emails, this one was actually refreshingly to the point. I caved. I thought perhaps he had seen the light and that we might get back together. But after a few weekends of seeing each other again, I realized that nothing had changed. Michael was still the "one day at a time" guy and wouldn't even commit to saying that we were seeing each other again.

It was around this time that I found an anonymous letter in my mailbox at work. The mysterious white envelope with my name handwritten on the outside contained an unsigned typed letter. The writer had seen the interview I had done about being a single Christian on the dating website ChristianCafe.com. I was blown away by his words:

Hi Wendy: I thought you were rather extraordinary in many ways even before I read your interview on ChristianCafe.com, but after reading it, I cannot for the life of me understand why someone hasn't snatched you up yet. And I agree—probably because guys are wimps. What is happening to my fellow men?! I noticed you right away on the *700 Club* years ago. Not only are you incredibly attractive, but you're intelligent, self-motivated, energetic, creative, courageous and gutsy. You look fantastic for being in your 40s. Your interview was great—speaking with absolute conviction. You obviously think men should be men. I love that phrase "Man up!" You are absolutely gorgeous and would be an incredible catch. I can't believe you're not married. But hang in there;

God will provide. Some lucky guy is out there. Keep up the great work! Thanks.

Wow. I was so moved that a man I'd never met, who apparently had no ulterior motives, would take the time to write a letter to compliment and encourage me in such a way and even to thank me! More importantly, I was startled to realize that this total stranger saw more value in me than the man I was currently dating did. In fact, Michael didn't seem to see any of the qualities in me that the letter writer had listed. Instead of celebrating who I was, he constantly told me, in a "you're not good enough" tone, to "do more, be more."

As I'd sensed when I had seen the "red herring" vanity plate, I had a strong conviction that the timing of this letter was from the Lord and that God was giving me a wakeup call. A loud one. It was as if the Lord were shouting, "Wendy, yes, these kinds of men do exist—men who will see what I see in you, men who will cherish you, men who will see your inner strength and beauty and will love you for who you really are. Don't settle!"

I couldn't resist reading the letter to Michael. "I think you need to hear this," I told him. It was a bold move, but I felt that I needed to share it. Michael took the challenge for a few days—but ladies, you can lead a horse to water, but you can't make it drink. You really can't change a man's heart, his character or his passion. Only God can do that. If a man doesn't see you as a prize to be won, as the treasure that God has given him, then he's not "the one." Shake the dust off your feet, and move on. God has more for you.

And let's face it. At some point, eating only crumbs will make us hungry as well as nauseous. But though we are weakened from being love starved, we must find the courage to move on.

In one of my favorite movies, *The Holiday*, actress Kate Winslet's character, Iris, escapes to sunny L.A. from cold and dreary England to get away from Jasper, the man who had broken her heart and whom she had just found out was engaged to another girl in her office. Jasper, used to having his cake and eating it too, decides to show up in L.A. unannounced. A surprised but happy Iris lets him in, thinking that surely he's no longer engaged. They're sitting on the couch getting cozy when, as Jasper leans in to kiss her, Iris has the presence of mind to ask, "So you are free to do this? You're not still engaged to be married, are you?"

Jasper looks at her and says, "I wish you could know how confusing this is for me."

Iris, understandably unhappy, replies, "Let me translate: You are still engaged to be married!" After realizing his answer is yes, she goes on to say, "You have never treated me right. Ever! . . . You broke my heart. And you acted like somehow it was my fault, my misunderstanding, and I was too in love with you to ever be mad at you, so I just punished myself! For years! But you waltzing in here on my lovely Christmas holiday, and telling me that you don't want to lose me whilst you're about to get MARRIED, somehow newly entitles me to say, it's over! This—this twisted, toxic thing between us, is finally finished! I'm miraculously done being in love with you! I've got a life to start living. And you're not going to be in it!"

Jasper shakes his head, not recognizing this new woman in front of him, and says, "What exactly has got into you?" Iris replies, "I don't know. But I think what I've got is something slightly resembling gumption!"[1] And she slams the door on the two-timing man.

It took Iris three years, but she finally realized that she'd been settling for crumbs the entire time, and now there was no way she would go back to that depleted dinner table. (In the long run, she ends up with a great guy who really loves her.)

Remember, a crumb is a "small particle of bread, cake, etc. that has broken off; a small portion of anything; fragment; bit."

Iris didn't settle for crumbs in the end, and you shouldn't either. God has a great big love for you, a full-size loaf, an entire cake filled with love and happiness! In fact, the whole inventory of the bakery is yours to be had, and do you know why? Because you are worth it! You're a daughter of the King! *You sit at the royal table with a multitude of delicacies.* Don't go back for crumbs unless you want to starve to death.

Prayer

Heavenly Father, please help Your daughters not to look back! Help us resist the temptation to go back to Crumbsville when You have set a royal table before us, a banqueting feast of love. Give us the strength, Lord, to stand on Your Word and Your truth that if we don't settle, You will give us your best and nothing less, and You "will do exceedingly abundantly above all that we ask or think" (Eph. 3:20). In Jesus' name, amen.

REFLECTIONS

1. Why is it so hard sometimes for us not to look back?
2. What does the Bible say about not looking back?
3. Why do we, like Kate Winslet's character Iris, sometimes settle for crumbs when God has so much more for us?

Note

1. Nancy Meyers, *The Holiday*, (2006). Quoted in IMDb http://www.imdb.com/title/tt0457939/quotes (accessed October 2013).

17

HEARTBREAK HOTEL

The LORD *is close to the brokenhearted and*
saves those who are crushed in spirit.
PSALM 34:18, *NIV*

Remember that popular song by the Eagles, "Hotel California," about a place where "you can check out any time you like, but you can never leave"?

Sometimes when our heart has been broken, it feels as if we will never leave Heartbreak Hotel. No matter how hard we try, no matter how many new haircuts, trips to exotic locations, talks with our girlfriends or promotions we get at work, that perpetual ache is still there, and the sadness is still in our eyes, hiding behind our forced smiles. We beg God over and over to take the pain, but like an unwanted guest, it remains, refusing to leave. And it has nearly convinced us that it never will.

But take heart, my dear sister. That's not what the Word of God says:

I waited patiently for the LORD; and He inclined to me, and heard my cry. *He also brought me up out of a horrible pit,* out of the miry clay, and set my feet upon a rock, and established my steps. *He has put a new song in my mouth*—praise to our God; many will see it and fear, and will trust in the LORD (Ps. 40:1-3, emphasis added).

If you've been mired in sorrow for any length of time, it's time to give heartbreak an eviction notice. *It's time for you to sing a new song.* The Lord God Almighty has heard your cry, daughter. He has seen your tears and declares to you today that He will repay you for all you have lost!

Say to those who are fearful-hearted, "Be strong, do not fear! Behold, your God will come with vengeance, with the recompense of God; He will come and save you" (Isa. 35:4).

Listen to the whispers of God. He has more for you; He's going to give you double for your trouble. He's going to reward you for your obedience in walking away from the good or the not so good so that He can bring you His best.

Did you know that there are certain things God always rewards? Obedience, for sure, but God also rewards our sorrow. The Bible says so:

Those who sow in tears shall reap in joy. He who continually goes forth weeping, bearing seed for sowing, shall doubtless come again with rejoicing, bringing his sheaves with him (Ps. 126:5-6).

Our tears are like liquid prayers that God holds in a bottle. He saves each precious, salty drop, and when the time is right, He turns our tears into sheer joy. Your heart will rejoice again, you will laugh again, and like the people in Psalm 126, you will declare God's goodness again.

When I was going through heartache, I made the password to my computer "Laughter." I wanted to remind myself every time I turned my computer on that I would laugh again, that my heart would rejoice again. I love Psalm 126, because it's a promise of joy and laughter after sorrow.

Read the entire psalm out loud, and stand on God's promises today:

When the LORD brought back the captivity of Zion, we were like those who dream. Then our mouth was filled with laughter, and our tongue with singing. Then they said among the nations, "The LORD has done great things for them." The LORD has done great things for us, and we are glad. Bring back our captivity, O Lord, as the streams in the South. Those who sow in tears shall reap in joy. He who continually goes forth weeping, bearing seed for sowing, shall doubtless come again with rejoicing, bringing his sheaves with him.

Daughter, your heartbreak is only for a season. It will not set up permanent residence in your home. God is too good to let that happen. When sorrow has finished its work in you, God will turn your pain into the greatest blessing you have ever known. And what you thought might destroy you will actually become your greatest strength. "And we know that all things [even your losses], work together for good to those who love God, to those who are the called according to His purpose" (Rom. 8:28). Charles Stanley puts it this way: "Every test, every trial, every heartache that's been significant, I can turn it over and see how God has turned it into good no matter what."

Hope in God

Why are you cast down, O my soul? And why are you disquieted within me? Hope in God; for I shall yet praise Him, the help of my countenance and my God (Ps. 43:5).

When we have experienced heartache that has been so agonizing and intense, it can be hard for us to trust God again. We may even blame

God for the horrible pain we have gone through. After all, didn't He allow us to go through it? But here's the good news: *The One who led you in will surely lead you out.* God is faithful to lead us in paths of righteousness, and He will provide the way of escape to rescue us and lead us out!

In Exodus chapter 14, we read that the Israelites were literally between a rock and hard place. The Egyptians were hot on their trail, and the people of Israel thought that God had surely abandoned them. But then—God did the impossible! With one obedient step of faith, Moses raised his trembling staff over the Red Sea, and voila! The waters rolled back, and the children of Israel walked through the sea on dry land! Just as quickly, the waters came back down, drowning and utterly destroying the Egyptians.

That's what God will do for you and me: The pain, the broken promises, the disappointment, the despair . . . God will wipe them out! What the enemy intended for our ultimate destruction, God Himself will turn around for our total victory, and as it was with Pharaoh's army, our sorrow will be no more. "Not one of them survived" (Exod. 14:28, *NIV*).

The Lord says to you, "Daughter, you are coming out! You are coming through! You are going to make it! Your past is buried, your enemies are defeated—I'm bringing you out stronger and better than before! Take heart! I'm the God who parted the Red Sea. Is anything too hard for Me?"

It's Not Your Fault

Sometimes when your pain stays with you well past what seems to be an appropriate time of mourning, it is because you're believing a lie about your situation. Marguerite Evans, speaker and minister as well as a friend of mine, says that sometimes the pain of heartbreak can be tied to something false we believe about ourselves or the relationship we've lost. "It is the lies that keep the pain alive," Evans says.

For example, even months after my breakup, my heartache was intense. I still played every detail of the past year over and over in my mind—every activity, every conversation—trying to figure out where things had gone wrong and what I could have done differently.

As Marguerite and I prayed together one day, I asked the Lord if I was believing anything that wasn't true. I immediately heard in my spirit the words, *It's my fault.* The Holy Spirit was revealing to me that the reason I was hurting so much is that I felt responsible—as if the demise of my relationship with Michael was *all my fault.* But that was a lie from the pit of hell! I repented for believing the lie and asked God to flood me with His truth and deliver me from this false responsibility.

I also forgave my ex-boyfriend for his part. After all, it takes two to hold a relationship together—well, three, actually, if you include the most important person: God. The truth was, I had loved Michael, I had given him my heart, I had done everything I knew to make the relationship work, and it still hadn't worked. Our breakup wasn't my fault. The relationship had simply ended, and I was not responsible.

After that breakthrough prayer with Marguerite, I still struggled with feelings of guilt, but thankfully, they weren't as intense. Eventually I embraced the truth that what had happened really wasn't my fault. I was walking out my healing, so to speak. It was so freeing.

It takes time to change a mindset—even a false one. Be patient with yourself. But whatever you do, don't buy the lie that if a relationship you were in didn't work out, it was all your fault. God is so much bigger than our mistakes. We can drive ourselves crazy trying to fix our errors in our minds, when in reality, there's no way we can fix things. Our bridges have burned, and there's no turning back. What happened is in the past. It's time to receive God's truth.

If you gave everything to a relationship that eventually failed, know that the breakup wasn't your fault, daughter. You did your best. You were loving, you were beautiful, you gave your all, and there's no shame in that. Forgive yourself, and forgive the man. God has something so much better for you. It's time for you to leave Heartbreak Hotel. Someday you'll wonder why you ever checked in.

You Are Precious to God

A dear friend of mine, Libby Starks, whom God graciously sent to help me walk through my own painful season, recently sent me this note of encouragement. I believe it's for you as well:

> Daughter, you are precious to God. He will never leave you nor forsake you. You are constantly on His mind, and He is working on your behalf. Train your mind on this, and release all your negative thoughts. *All is well.* In fact, one day you will look over your shoulder and wonder what the big deal was. Don't worry. Be happy. Love is just around the corner!
>
> Love, Libby

"He heals the brokenhearted and binds up their wounds. He counts the number of the stars; He calls them all by name" (Ps. 147:3-4). The God who counts the stars and knows them all by name is the same God who right now is reaching in and healing your broken heart. Trust Him. He loves you so much. He is leading you out of a horrible pit, and soon, very soon, you'll be looking over your shoulder with a smile and wondering what the big deal was. Your feet will be back on solid ground.

Today is a new day!

Alison's Story

Trust me, no matter what you've been through, God can turn it around for your good. My good friend Alison is a testament to that fact.

One day Alison got the phone call that no wife ever wants to get: "Your husband is missing." The good news is that God had prepared her for the worst—and now He's preparing her for His best. This is Alison's story of heartache and hope.

From the outside looking in, my marriage looked like any other with its normal ups and downs. But the truth is, the extremes of those ups and downs were anything but normal. Looking back now over the 19 years of our union, it was only by the grace of God that I survived the roller coaster we were on.

From the beginning, our relationship was unpredictable. We married young; I was 24 and John was 25. John was handsome and at times could be incredibly sweet and charming. He had a way of making a stranger into a friend in minutes, and no one could tell a story like he could. He was strong and protective. When he was up, he was my best friend. But I never knew which John would walk through the door at the end of the day: the happy John, the depressed and withdrawn John or the angry, blaming John. Living with a man who suffered from an undiagnosed chemical imbalance, most likely bipolar disorder, challenged me daily. For years I worked hard to meet his needs, trying to make him happy, trying to make him see how much I loved him. Meanwhile, I was clueless about the fact that he was having countless extramarital affairs behind my back.

Each day I prayed, *Lord, please save my husband! Have mercy on him, and heal his heart.*

How amazing that all the while, the Lord was healing mine! He was calling me to a life fully dependent on Him, and I began to see that in order for my family to be what God wanted it to be, I had to give Jesus all of me! I had to devote myself to being as close to the Lord as I could possibly get. He knew, even then, just how much I was soon going to need Him and He had a plan for my survival: *Him!* I knew that God loved John unconditionally, so I began to seek the Lord's heart and eyes to love and see John as He did. Yet my prayers were self-serving, as I clung to the idea that when John accepted Christ, all our troubles would be over, and then I'd be loved by my husband the way I had always dreamed I'd be.

As I daily, sometimes moment by moment, sought Jesus' heart and eyes for John, I began to realize how much my focus and my prayers were about me and how difficult my life was. I had been asking Jesus to work in John's heart and to change him so that I would be loved and my life would be better. Then one day the Lord asked me, "If John never changes, will I be enough for you?" God's wisdom behind challenging me with this question astounds me even today. He truly knows what we need!

At the time, I hated that question. I didn't think it was fair. *Why wouldn't God open my husband's eyes to see how he'd been treating me?* After all, wouldn't it help John as well? I wrestled with this until it drove me to my knees, where I saw my selfishness and my limited view of God. I had to admit that I wasn't sure that God was enough. I begged Him to move in my heart as the lover of my soul and to help me know that I could trust Him with all my needs. I said yes to His plans for my life, and that was all He needed! Grace swept in and made the impossible possible! My heart began to shift as I fell more in love with Jesus.

I began to hear His words about me, how much He loved me and valued me. I began to see the big picture about my life from a heavenly perspective. My life was no longer focused on me and on getting my needs met by a man, because Jesus was fulfilling my needs. My life became first about my relationship with Jesus and second about loving my husband with Jesus' love. I had the privilege and the honor of loving John just as he was. In the goodness of God, I had Jesus' heart and eyes for John, and I saw so many beautiful things in my husband. My children amazed me and loved their father with this same pure love.

Thanks to my loving Father, my foundation was firmly in place. Still, nothing could have prepared me for the day my daughters came home saying, "Mom, Dad took us out today and told us he received Christ! But Mom, Dad said that Marilyn is the one who led him to the Lord." The words hit me with a powerful punch as I realized the full impact of what that meant, and my daughter's tears of grief made me realize that she knew as well!

Suddenly, everything began to make sense—John's long phone calls out on our back deck, all his late nights "at the office," my friend Marilyn acting jumpy and nervous around me. I could almost hear the devil's pleasure as I writhed in the realization that my good Christian friend was having an affair with my husband. This was the moment, *the* moment we'd been praying for for years: John's salvation! And here it was, wrapped in gut-wrenching grief. How could this be happening? Then the words from my husband's lips, "I don't love you anymore," drove the stake even deeper into my heart. Despite my devotion and my determination that my family would be all that God intended it to be, our life together was ending.

For the first time in my life, the D word was used. "I want a divorce" cut like a knife into my heart. John was through with our marriage. That was it; it was over. God had known all along that I would need Him so deeply in my heart to walk out these next months as my husband's countless other affairs were revealed. John's mood swings and depression grew more severe. Reasoning with him became impossible. Then the phone call came Easter Sunday night, April 4, 2010: "John is missing." My whole world seemed to be upside down.

Calls from detectives who were searching for my husband came daily for four days and then this call from my sister-in-law: "They found him. He shot himself. John is dead." Where was the ground under my feet? How could it be true that I was a widow? And how would I be able to raise my girls on my own? How could I possibly keep putting one foot in front of the other and walk out a life that looked nothing like what I had dreamed it would back when I was a 24-year-old newlywed?!

But God! God had so established His place in my heart and my place in His. All the work He'd done in me over the previous years helped me to hang on to His hand. Every morning He met me when I woke up, pouring grace and mercy into my girls and me as He loved our hearts back to wholeness.

Now, three years later, I know without a doubt that the Lord has someone incredibly special for me. Jesus has taught me that I'm valuable and should be cherished by a man who sees in me what He sees in me. Settling for less than God's best for me is not an option that I will ever entertain. I will wait on my future husband while I wait on God to give me the desires of my heart! Jesus says I'm worth it! I am a prize to be won!

If God can heal Alison, He can heal you too. If you're going through heartbreak right now, pray this prayer:

Prayer

Father, I bring You my broken heart. You're the maker of hearts, and You're the only One who can fix me. I want to leave Heartbreak Hotel—rescue me from this pain. Thank You that You rescued me from what could have been a terrible fate. Although my heart is broken, You have promised to fix it and to give me exuberant joy [see Ps. 126]. I release this heartache and pain to You, and I release to You the one who caused it. I lay my every anxiety, fear and worry at Your feet. I trust You, Jesus. I know that You will turn everything around for my good. Help me to trust You with my whole heart again. I love you, Father. In Jesus' name, amen.

REFLECTIONS

1. Does God promise to heal the brokenhearted?
2. Do you believe that those who "sow in tears shall reap in joy" (Ps. 126:5)?
3. In Romans 8:28 God promises that "all things work together for good," even heartache. Has this been true in your life? Have you experienced this?

18

UNLIKELY HEALERS

Men are the enemy, but I still love the enemy.
RENÉE ZELLWEGER IN *JERRY MAGUIRE*

When a man breaks our heart, it can be highly tempting for us to make all men the enemy. In the movie *Jerry Maguire*, there is a scene in which a group of divorced women get together to support one another, and they seemingly place all men into the enemy category. But that's really not fair to the male species, is it? Women break hearts too—all the time, in fact. If truth be told, I know that I'm not innocent of breaking a few, and you probably aren't either.

If we live long enough, we're bound to get our heart broken somewhere along the line—and maybe it's an experience we should all go through. I know that before I had my heart broken, I never understood the pain that divorced people went through or the grief of losing a loved one. I am a bit closer to understanding that pain now. Even though I wasn't married, when my relationship with Michael ended, it felt like a divorce, like a breaking, like a ripping away. It felt like a death. And it was a death—the death of a relationship. But I discovered, and hopefully you have or will discover soon, that there is life after death, even the death of a beloved relationship.

Jesus told Martha, "I am the resurrection and the life. He who believes in Me, though he may die, he shall live" (John 11:25). He also says, "I make all things new" (Rev. 21:5).

Jesus promises to turn our ashes that seem to have no value into something so beautiful that we won't believe our eyes. He understands what we're going through. He's been there. He felt the rejection and the betrayal, and He endured the cross—the most shameful method of execution in biblical times—for you and for me. Those feelings of despair after heartbreak, divorce or any type of devastation in our lives are only temporary. All things will be new!

Trust Jesus. He's the God who specializes in resurrection. No other god has ever claimed to have been raised from the dead. Our Lord knows what He's talking about.

Men Can Be Healers

In the days, weeks and months after my breakup, I discovered something really wonderful about men. While a certain man in my life had undoubtedly been the cause of great pain and heartache, God used other men as part of my healing.

First, there was my own father, Kelly Griffith, who has been my biggest fan since I can remember. Whether it was an elementary school play, cheerleading tryouts in high school, my decision to go into journalism during college, my first television job across the country in Yuma, Arizona at the age of 23 or my eventual decision to apply for a job with CBN, my dad has always been behind me 100 percent. When I told my dad how I felt after Michael and I broke up, he held me, my tears falling on his shoulder, and told me as he had so many times before, "You are special." Then, after this brief moment of pure sensitivity, he got really angry that someone had broken my heart! It's a dad thing, and I loved it.

Then there was Dr. Pat Robertson, head of CBN but also one of my greatest spiritual advisors, who had asked me to share with him my story, as he knew I was hurting. He echoed my father's words,

"You are special," and then added the phrase that partly inspired this book: "Don't throw yourself away."

And I'll never forget when CBN news director Rob Allman looked me in the eyes and gave me the inspirational words I desperately needed moments before show time. As tears rolled down my cheeks, he said to me, "Wendy, you're stronger than you know." And he was right, even though I didn't feel strong. Never before had the words "the show must go on" meant more to me than they did that afternoon. God gave me the strength to wipe away my tears and to do my job when the cameras started rolling.

God works in interesting ways, and He provides avenues for our survival. Having to be on camera every day—which meant, of course, having to put on makeup, fix my hair, dress nicely and get to the studio on time—was more of a gift than I could have realized. I needed to be focused on my work during those days, and God made sure that I was.

Working at CBN in itself was a great blessing, because I was able to get lost in my work while being surrounded by wonderful, supportive, godly people. I'm so thankful for my amazing male co-anchors Lee Webb, George Thomas and Mark Martin, who were great brothers and who encouraged me by always modeling true manliness and godliness.

CBN news producer Drew Parkhill, a great friend of mine for over a decade (and whom I pray has special rewards in heaven for being such a great listener), is also someone I must mention as being a true rock for me during my time of heartache. Drew, a great encourager and confidant, literally saved my life (okay, not literally, but he was the person I called when I was at my lowest points, and he always found a way to cheer me up). Weekends were hard for me after the breakup, and sometimes going to a movie with Drew helped me feel alive again. Thank you, Drew Parkhill! Your friendship means more than you'll ever know.

And of course my real brothers, Truman and Pete Griffith, helped me on the road to healing. They have always been nice to any guy I've ever dated and have always given him the benefit of the doubt, so when my relationship with Michael was over, they said to me, "Well, there's only one explanation for this, Wendy. He's obviously gay." Michael was definitely not gay, but their words made me laugh and made me realize that my brothers were definitely on my side.

In fact, it's been a delight to have my brother Truman's insights as I've written this book. Truman, a 36-year-old attorney and father of two, accidentally turned out to be the perfect copy editor for my book when I asked him to read a few chapters. He gave me some good feedback, and it was great to have a man's perspective on a book that is written mostly for women. Inspired by some of the book's chapters, Truman (whose name means "faithful man") wrote me the following email during the writing/editing process. He added a bit to it for insertion in the book, as I felt compelled to include it:

Wendy,

Just a few thoughts. After reading some of your chapters and seeing what you went through with Michael, I want you to know, as your brother, how very sorry I am that this happened to you. You deserve so much better. But I pray that you will understand that all men are not the enemy.

I can't help but be reminded of the following famous words of Jesus: *"Father, forgive them, for they do not know what they do"* (Luke 23:34). Of course, Jesus was asking for forgiveness for those who had nailed Him to a cross to die and who were mocking Him as He suffered. I think many men, including me, would say the following when reflecting on a past relationship: *"Father, forgive me. I was a compete jerk and had no idea what I was doing at the time."* I say this because I, like most men I know, have done things I regret in my past relationships, and I'm not sure I really thought about or had the maturity level to think about what I was doing. (But don't get me wrong—I take full responsibility for all my actions!)

I've been a complete jerk, and at times I've not given women the respect they deserved. I've made a thousand and one mistakes when it comes to relationships. And this is coming from a guy who loves, respects and has a great relationship with his mom and his three older sisters and also has an older brother who told me exactly what *not* to do and how *not* to act. So if anyone should know from a young age exactly how to treat and respect members of the opposite sex, it's me. But unfortunately, it took time. Despite all the good advice I received, I had to make all my own mistakes in high school and college, break a few hearts (or at least make some girls pretty upset), have my own heart broken a few times, endure plenty of slaps to the face and, most importantly, live with the looks on the faces of women whom I knew I had saddened because I didn't value them properly.

I think it's typical for a lot of young men to think something better is always out there. I, like most men, I think, had an entitlement complex that I could have a girlfriend and not take it that seriously because I was young and was put on this earth to experience all that life had to offer. I still have a ton of guilt from living the entitlement lifestyle as a young man, and I plan to talk to my son about how not to live that way. Let's hope he is better at taking advice than his dad was.

I have no doubt that that's why God gave me a daughter at a young age—to learn to truly love and respect women. I truly do now, as you know. (My wife may laugh at my self-serving words, but I think at the end of the day she's pretty happy with me!)

My point is, *men can change*, and sometimes a man with a not-so-great track record is exactly the guy you need to give a first-date chance to. You want to find a guy whose mistakes have been made and who has learned his lessons, not a guy whose mistakes are still around the corner. Yes, even Michael could show up a changed man, having recognized his mistakes. Obviously he came back once, and you gave him a second chance, and you quickly realized that he was no different. That was your responsibility, and you did a good job of recognizing it.

That brings me to my second point, which you have touched on but may not truly get because you are not a man: *Men are transparent.* Our actions and words will tell you exactly what you need to know. If we say we are not ready to settle down at this point in our life, then most likely what we're really saying is, "We don't truly love and value you," and you should run! We are looking for another woman who is worthy of us settling down with. If we say we aren't comfortable talking about the future, then you are simply not the one for us (and we probably have no intention of marrying you—at least you should hope we don't). If we say "I love you but . . . ," as your friend Michael said to you, you are simply a layover on our flight to somewhere else. We are looking for something else, something better (in our opinion), something that is most certainly not you.

Those are the words, but what about the actions? You touch on it in the book. If we don't pick up the check on the first couple dates, then you are a friend, not a love interest. If we stop calling unexpectedly and blame it on being busy at work—c'mon, is anyone falling for that anymore? Here's a great one: We say that we are not going out tonight, then you proceed to say that you are going to a certain place or function, then we stutter and now say that we may actually go to that same place or function—that means that we had plans to go to that place or function all along, just without you. Some women will think, *Well, he is going to that place or function now because I am going;* but if that were the case, wouldn't he have asked you to go with him in the first place instead of saying he was staying in? It's all quite simple.

A man shows the signs, and the woman has to pick up on them. If the signs are bad, the woman has to escape immediately. If the woman does not send the guy packing at any of those points, she is in a very real way enabling his "bad guy" behavior, and he may never learn the lessons of real manhood.

The point is this: Get rid of a man who doesn't truly value you. By doing so, you obviously help yourself, but you may also help some other woman who has to deal with that guy in the future. (I'm sure my wife is truly thankful to all the women who put me in my place for being a jerk to them!) There is simply no perfect guy out there, but there are guys out there who have been imperfect in the past and now know what *not* to do. And that guy may be the perfect guy for you! So be ready to give some other guys a chance.

Anyway, just some thoughts.

Love ya,

Truman

Prayer

Lord, thank You for the men in our lives. Bless them to be the strong leaders, providers and protectors that You've called them to be. Raise up strong men of faith who will desire to be husbands and fathers to one woman whom they will cherish and love for a lifetime. At the same time, help us to understand that men are transparent. Enable us to pick up on their signals and to know when a man is truly serious about us or only taking us for a ride. In Jesus' name, amen.

REFLECTIONS

1. Can you identify men who have had a positive influence on your life and your relationships?
2. Why are men important in our healing process?
3. Why is it important for us to realize that just because one man hurt us, not all men are the enemy?

19

BEGIN AGAIN

On a Wednesday in a cafe, I watched it begin again.
TAYLOR SWIFT FROM "BEGIN AGAIN"

It was right after New Year's, almost a year since my initial breakup with Michael, but only a few months since we had last seen each other and tried to work things out. Although I was trying desperately to move on, Michael was still consuming my thoughts, and my heart was heavy. "Lord, when will I be free from this heartache?" I prayed. "It's been almost a year."

As I made the long and winding journey along I-64 West from my parent's home in West Virginia to my home in Virginia Beach, the radio landed on Taylor Swift's new song, "Begin Again," and the lyrics took my breath away. (You might want to take a minute and download the song and give it a listen.) This song illustrated my life at this time, even the part where Taylor mentions that her old boyfriend never thought she was funny.

And when she sang "on a Wednesday in a cafe, I watched it begin again,"[1] I burst into tears. I was almost heaving, the words hit my soul so hard. I heard the song several more times during the eight-hour ride home, and each time she got to the part, "I watched it begin again," I would burst into tears! *Why am I crying?* I wondered.

After being puzzled at my emotional reaction to the lyrics, I finally figured out what I was feeling: *hope!* There was so much *hope* in this song. Swift was singing about new beginnings and about how love can happen when we're least expecting it, even during the middle of the week, on a Wednesday, when we pop into Starbucks or wherever for our afternoon coffee. And interestingly, like my former boyfriend, the guy she sang about hadn't thought she was funny—but her new beau did! It felt as if she knew my story somehow and was singing just for me. (And just for the record, I have a great sense of humor and love to laugh, ask almost anyone, except you know who.)

God wanted me to hope again, even to hope for a new love—in fact, I needed to be what the Bible calls a prisoner of hope: "Return to the stronghold, you prisoners of hope. Even today I declare that I will restore double to you" (Zech. 9:12).

When we're a prisoner to something, there's no escaping from it. I didn't want to be a prisoner of despair or sorrow—no, I wanted to be a prisoner of hope. I wanted to be like Abraham who, regarding God's promise, "hoped against hope" (see Rom. 4:18). Being a prisoner of hope means that no matter what things look like in the natural, no matter how true it was that I had spent another New Year's Eve without a significant other or was facing another Valentine's Day without a true love, I can hope and believe that God has not forgotten me.

> Though the fig tree may not blossom, nor fruit be on the vines; though the labor of the olive may fail, and the fields yield no food; though the flock may be cut off from the fold, and there be no herd in the stalls—yet I will rejoice in the LORD. I will joy in the God of my salvation (Hab. 3:17-18).

"Begin Again" details a girl's new start with a new, appreciative love interest. Swift, who debuted the tune on *Good Morning America*, explained, "It's actually a song about when you've gotten through a really bad relationship, and you finally dust yourself off and go on that first date after a horrible breakup,"[1] she said. Unfortunately for the young Swift, it appears that she's already had plenty of experience with "dusting herself off" after heartbreak. But at least she's able to turn her pain into some really great songs that I know have blessed and encouraged a lot of people like me.

Just as Swift sings about in her songs, God loves to turn our pain into something beautiful and to give us a fresh start:

> Do not remember the former things, nor consider the things of old. Behold, I will do a new thing, now it shall spring forth; shall you not know it? I will even make a road in the wilderness and rivers in the desert (Isa. 43:18-19).

New Beginnings

Whether you are divorced, widowed or devastated from a recent breakup, there is a new beginning in your future. God has not forgotten you. You will be able to love again. You, daughter of the Most High King, are worthy of love—worthy of a great love! It's my experience that whatever sacrifice you go through for God, He will repay you for your pain. And when God repays us, He always gives us something better than what we had before. A pastor I know once said, "What you are willing to walk away from determines what God is willing to bring to you."

Do you need to walk away from something that's not good for you, perhaps even a relationship that's causing you pain? If you do it, I believe that God will give you something better. God promises to give us the desires of our heart if we delight in Him (see Ps. 37:4). There is hope on the other side of letting go. And this is what is so cool: Even if our loss happened because of our own ignorance or sin, God is so loving and merciful that His word promises that He will restore all your losses. I love Joel 2:25-27:

> I will restore to you the years that the swarming locust has eaten, the crawling locust, the consuming locust, and the chewing locust, my great army which I sent among you. You shall eat in plenty and be satisfied, and praise the name of the LORD your God, who has dealt wondrously with you; and My people shall never be put to shame.
>
> Then you shall know that I am in the midst of Israel: I am the LORD your God and there is no other. My people shall never be put to shame.

My sister JeanAnne and I love to quote this passage. As I shared earlier, JeanAnne had to kiss a lot of frogs before she met her prince. Many of the guys she dated didn't see her true value, and she would call me in tears, wondering what to do. She had her heart severely broken when she was in her early 20s. She had given her whole heart to a man she thought was "the one." When it didn't work out, she was devastated. It took her years to find her confidence again, but she never gave up hope.

JeanAnne went on to become an international flight attendant and was always jetting off to exotic destinations like Paris, Rome or one of the Caribbean islands. With her busy traveling schedule, she didn't have much time to date, so she went on Match.com and a few other sites. Once again, she had to kiss a few frogs—well, endure a few bad dates anyway—and even put up with some mean dates when she met guys who told her, "You don't look like your picture." My sister is beautiful and has done a fair bit of modeling, so clearly those guys were blind. Still, even in the face of rejection, my sister never gave up hope of finding true love.

She continued to grow spiritually and to prepare herself to be a bride. She studied books on dating and on marriage and was active in ladies' Bible studies. Finally, one day she met a guy on Match.com named Paul. Reluctant but willing to give things another try, JeanAnne agreed to meet him at a local Starbucks for their first date. When she

walked in, he was sitting at a table, waiting for her to arrive. When
Paul saw my sister, he stood up, and she observed his full six-foot-
four muscular frame for the first time. That's when she heard herself
say, "I finally hit the jackpot."

Paul quickly differentiated himself from the other men JeanAnne
had gone out with. He was what she called a prepared man. He had
a good job, was financially secure and was ready to husband a wife.
Many guys today are only playing with the idea of marriage—literally
"playing house" with no intention of making a commitment. Paul
was also a strong God-fearing Catholic, and he was a man's man.
As her older sister by eleven and a half months (we're Irish twins),
I overwhelmingly approved.

JeanAnne politely let Paul know that at her age, she wasn't on the
five-year plan. That's not being pushy—it's simply letting a guy know
that he needs to make up his mind sooner, rather than later, if you're
the one for him. And after dating for a year and a half, JeanAnne and
Paul set a wedding date for May 20. She was 40 years old, he was 38.

JeanAnne was the most beautiful bride I've ever seen. The years
of waiting for her prince had only made her more radiant. As she
walked down the aisle, she looked no more than 29. She and Paul
both did.

They honeymooned on the coast of Italy. A year later God blessed them with a beautiful healthy baby boy, who was followed by
a gorgeous, Italian-looking, dark-haired baby girl when my sister
was 43. God did indeed restore the years that the locusts had eaten.
In fact, JeanAnne says she enjoys being a mom in her 40s much more
than she would have in her 30s when she was jet-setting all over the
world as an international flight attendant. Now she's able to stay
home with the kids, and she says she wouldn't have it any other way.

God Will Restore

If God did it for my sister, He can do it for you and for me. He is the
God of the turnaround. Just ask Job.

The book of Job is a difficult one. Job was a righteous man who loved God—yet He had everything he held dear taken from him: his family, his health, his riches and his friends. Yet, because he kept the right spirit, held onto his faith and even maintained hope—"Though He slay me, yet I will hope in him" (Job 13:15, *NIV*) was his declaration—God restored everything to him.

> And the LORD restored Job's losses when he prayed for his friends. Indeed the LORD gave Job twice as much as he had before. Then all his brothers, all his sisters, and all those who had been his acquaintances before, came to him and ate food with him in his house; and they consoled him and comforted him for all the adversity that the LORD had brought upon him. Each one gave him a piece of silver and each a ring of gold.
>
> Now the LORD blessed the latter days of Job more than his beginning; for he had fourteen thousand sheep, six thousand camels, one thousand yoke of oxen, and one thousand female donkeys. He also had seven sons and three daughters. And he called the name of the first Jemimah, the name of the second Keziah, and the name of the third Keren-Happuch. In all the land were found no women so beautiful as the daughters of Job; and their father gave them an inheritance among their brothers.
>
> After this Job lived one hundred and forty years, and saw his children and grandchildren for four generations. So Job died, old and full of days (Job 42:10-17).

As there was for Job, there is hope in your future. Hopefully none of us will experience the great losses that Job went through, although we will probably all experience some sort of loss. The great news is this: God loves to restore. He's an expert in rebuilding, renewing and resurrecting. He's an expert in new beginnings!

As I wrote this, I felt the Lord saying to me,

There is hope in your future. You will not be ashamed, daughter. You are worthy of a great love. No more compromise, no more settling for second best—you are a prize to be won. Don't settle for less than God's best. As Taylor Swift sings, "it's time to begin again."

As I continued driving on I-64 toward Virginia Beach, I no longer felt sad. I felt hope! Make no mistake about it, God speaks through music, and He was speaking to me during that long ride home, "Love is just around the corner, Wendy. When you least expect it, when you're not even looking for it, there he'll be, smiling from across the room, maybe holding a cup of coffee in his hand. And oh, yeah—he'll think you're hilarious."

Prayer

Father, thank you for hope! Where would we be without hope? Lord, give your daughters hope that the best is still yet to come—and that you are the God who delights to restore the years that the locust ate! We declare and decree that a new beginning is on the way—it's time to begin again. In Jesus' name, amen.

REFLECTIONS

1. Why is hope so powerful, especially in our seasons of mourning?
2. How do you begin again after a breakup?
3. What does God say about new beginnings?

20

PACK YOUR BAGS, AND I'LL DO THE REST

[God] is able to do exceedingly abundantly above all that we ask or think, according to the power that works in us.
EPHESIANS 3:20

I believe that everything good that comes to us in life, whether it's a new mindset, a new job or the person we hope to spend the rest of our lives with, comes to us by faith: "Now faith is the substance of things hoped for, the evidence of things not seen" (Heb. 11:1).

God told Abraham that he would have a son of his own, and Abraham took God at His word.

> And behold, the word of the LORD came to him, saying, "This one [your servant] shall not be your heir, but one who will come from your own body shall be your heir." Then He brought him outside and said, "Look now toward heaven, and count the stars if you are able to number them." And He said to him, "So shall your descendants be."

And he believed in the LORD, and He accounted it to him for righteousness (Gen. 15:4-6).

When God tells you that there is hope in your future, believe Him. When God tells you that you will be healed, believe Him. When God tells you that He has a wonderful husband for you, believe Him. Your faith is precious to God, and it will be rewarded.

Several years ago my faith was greatly rewarded when I heard the voice of the Lord speak these words to me during a time of prayer:

Pack your bags, and I'll do the rest.

It was a cold February night in 2007, and I was dreaming of escaping to some exotic warm land, perhaps Hawaii. As I've mentioned before, hiking is a serious passion of mine, and I had heard that Hawaii was a primo destination for some of the most spectacular hiking in the world.

I had actually started doing a little research on the subject and found out that one of the best hikes with the most incredible views was on the island of Kauai, which is also known as the Garden Isle because it's so lush and green.

That night, I was up in my prayer loft at my house talking to God about several things, including a vacation, when I clearly heard in my spirit this phrase: *Pack your bags, and I'll do the rest.* I knew that it was God. I don't know exactly how I knew, but I knew. I was so excited. But packing for Hawaii meant that I needed to go shopping, because I literally didn't have any vacation attire—no shorts, bathing suits, sundresses (sad but true—it had been that long since I had taken a real beach vacation).

And so my faith journey to Hawaii began that night with the Lord's simple command to me to pack my bags. I decided to take Him at His word, and that meant only one thing—shopping!

My first stop at the mall was J. Crew. I usually never shop there, but I was drawn to the casual, comfortable outfits on display in the store's colorful window.

I bought two of everything: two pairs of shorts, two pairs of linen pants, a green halter sundress and a black one, two bathing suits, a couple tank tops, two T-shirts and a bandana for hiking and a floppy straw hat. It was one of those anointed shopping times when everything fit perfectly and looked great. When all was said and done, I had spent exactly 700 dollars to the penny. That was a lot of money for me to spend at one time, but I knew that it was some sort of sign from God, since seven is the number of completion—so I must have really completed things! I couldn't wait to get home and start packing.

About two weeks later, March 15 to be exact, my dear friends from Kentucky, Pastor Doug and Linda Abner, were visiting me. I told them what the Lord had told me—"Pack your bags, and I'll do the rest." I showed Linda my suitcase that was neatly packed with all my new clothes for Hawaii, and I asked her if she would join me in prayer on the matter. As an act of faith, we laid hands on my suitcase and asked the Lord to reveal the next piece to the puzzle.

That night I had a dream. In the dream I saw a woman whom I know from my hometown at a pool. I walked over to her, and she told me that she was going to Hawaii from July 22 through August 4. I said to her, "I'm going too! I've already packed my bags, and I didn't know when I was going—but now I do!" Then I woke up.

As I woke from the dream, I kept repeating to myself, "July 22 to August 4," so I wouldn't forget the dates. I was certain that God had supernaturally spoken to me in that dream and had given me the dates for the trip, even though I couldn't remember ever receiving that kind of information in a dream before. I jumped out of bed to find a calendar. I wasn't sure how many days or weeks those days covered or if the timeframe started on a Monday or a Wednesday. When I looked at the calendar, I saw that the dates covered exactly two weeks from Sunday, July 22, to Saturday, August 4.

August was still four and a half months away—which I rationalized gave me just enough time to meet someone and get married. At that point I wasn't ruling anything out. I thought that the Lord must have me leaving on a Sunday because I was going to be married on Saturday, July 21, and my incredible, hiking-loving husband and I would leave for our honeymoon the next day. (Obviously, the whole wedding and husband thing was not yet in God's plans, but that doesn't ruin the story—so keep reading!)

The day after I had the dream, I filled out my time-off request form at work: "Wendy will be on summer vacation from July 22 to August 4." It was a big step of faith, but I had decided to take God at His word.

My Wait—and God's Answers

Then my real waiting began. I'd packed my bags, I knew *when* I was going, but I didn't know how I was going to get there or where I'd be staying. I waited for my next dream or word from the Lord. The rest of March, all of April and all of May, I heard nothing from God. Only silence.

By early June, I was starting to get nervous. *Lord, You gave me the dates, but where do You want me to stay?* I kept reminding the Lord that He had promised that if I packed my bags, He would take care of the rest. In the meantime, I had been doing some online research. I knew that the ideal part of Hawaii for me would be on the North Coast of Kauai. That's where the famous Na Pali cliffs are, with the best hiking on the islands. It was, unfortunately, also the most expensive part of Kauai, with the resort rooms running about 300 to 400 dollars a night or more.

I began to pray, and the Lord reminded me of my good friend Janie who had been to Hawaii—the same friend I previously stayed with in Kansas when I visited IHOP-KC. So I emailed Janie and told her about my plans, and I asked her if she could recommend any place to stay in Hawaii.

It turns out that when Janie had visited Hawaii, she had stayed on Kauai, the very island I was hoping to visit, and she graciously gave me the email address of the couple with whom she had stayed.

So I emailed Scott and Vicky Vanderhoof. I told them about our mutual friend Janie and gave them the dates I'd be coming to the islands. Then I asked if they could recommend a hotel or a place for me to stay on the island that wasn't too expensive since I was going to be there for two weeks.

The husband, Scott, emailed me back right away. Remember, he didn't know me from Adam. His was one of the most incredible and memorable emails I had ever received. Scott wrote,

> Wendy, if our house is available, you can have the house for free! Kauai is the most beautiful and undeveloped of the Hawaiian Islands, and the North Shore of Kauai is the most lush. We are leaving the morning of the 23rd of July.
>
> God is showing you His extravagant love for you! Seeing His extravagance will forever change you, how you live, how you love and how you worship Him.
>
> Get ready for some beauty and some rest. Whoopee! Our house has one of the best views in the entire Hawaiian Islands, overlooking the Hanalei Bay where they filmed South Pacific. You can see 180 degrees of green mountains with waterfalls. Your (heavenly) Father is rich and extravagant, and He will take care of things.
>
> Aloha! Scott

Amazingly, their home was on the Kauai's north shore, not far from the magnificent Na Pali Coast where I was hoping to hike.

Then Scott's wife Vicky emailed me. And if you don't believe in the supernatural yet, hopefully you will after this. Vicky wrote,

> Wendy, we received a prophetic word (about the same time you received the dates to travel from the Lord) that someone was going to visit our house this summer for a vacation.
>
> We had already planned to be in California on the dates you are visiting. *You're the one we've been expecting!*

Wow! This was all happening by the Spirit of God! So now, thanks to my friend Janie and this supernatural connection with Scott and Vicky, I had a place to stay. And not a beach shack but a home set on a cliff overlooking a million-dollar view of Hanalei Bay! Don't even try to figure out how expensive a place like that would be to rent for two weeks in Hawaii—and I was getting to stay there for free! Okay, I looked it up. Two weeks in Hawaii at a resort overlooking the Hanalei Bay would have cost me about five grand, so I was pretty excited, to say the least!

All I needed now was a plane ticket. So I began to search online. Everything was over a thousand dollars. After researching my options, I chose a flight and was about to push the "confirm" tab on my computer for a non-refundable ticket to Honolulu on Travelocity, when unexpectedly I heard the Lord say, "Do you want to buy it, or do you want Me to buy it?" I told Him, "I want *You* to buy it!" I was suddenly reminded again of what the Lord had originally told me: "Pack your bags, and I'll do the rest."

Even after God had supernaturally provided the exact dates and an amazing place for me to stay, I still didn't see how God was going to provide a plane ticket for me (me of little faith). So I put out a fleece: "Lord," I prayed, "even though every day the tickets are getting more expensive, I'm going to wait until Friday to hear from You on how to proceed." So when Friday came and I still didn't have a ticket, I got back online and once again came close to pressing the "confirm" button to buy a non-refundable Travelocity ticket.

Suddenly, I felt as if I should check with Delta. I knew that I had racked up a few SkyMiles in the past, but I had no idea how many I had or whether or not they were still viable. I gave Delta a call. "Yes, Miss Griffith, you have 80,000 SkyMiles, and you only need 70,000 to go to Hawaii. Your ticket is free."

God had done it again! The Holy Spirit hadn't let me buy that ticket because God had really meant what He said back in February when I was on my knees praying for a vacation. *Pack your bags, and I'll do the rest.*

So now I had the exact dates of travel, a place to stay and a plane ticket. I began to think that something pretty important and wonderful was awaiting me in the land of rainbows.

God's Rewards

When July 22 finally rolled around, I'm embarrassed to admit that I almost missed my flight out of Norfolk, Virginia.

You would think that after all this I would have gotten to the airport early, but I didn't. My flight was scheduled to leave at 6:20 a.m., and I didn't get to the airport until about 5:40 a.m. The usually quiet airport was packed with dozens of people trying to check their bags all at once at the sidewalk check-in.

The Sky-Cab attendant told me that I would never make it, but God gave me favor with him, and he checked the schedule for me one more time. He said, "You made the 30-minute pre-boarding requirement by 30 seconds!"

Praise Jesus! When I got to Honolulu, I had to catch another flight to Kauai, where I was told the same thing by one of the airline attendants: "You're not going to make your connection!" But once again God gave me favor with fellow travelers and with security, and I was able to cut in line. I made the flight!

Man, something really good must be waiting for me on Kauai if I'm going through all this, I thought.

When I arrived in Kauai, a little tired but super excited, I thought I was going to be on my own for the next two weeks—well, just me and Jesus. I was ready for some rest, so I wasn't worried about traveling alone.

I rented a green Chrysler Sebring convertible, put the top down and headed toward Scott and Vicky's home on the North Shore.

The drive was beautiful, and it made me even more excited to get to my destination. That night I got to meet Scott. He wouldn't be leaving to join his wife in California until the next day.

Scott and Vicky's home was hidden off the main road, but when I pulled into their driveway, I saw the majestic view that Scott had described: lush green mountains dripping with waterfalls and the deep blue of the ocean. I had to pinch myself to make sure I was still alive.

I arrived around dinner time. Scott had invited his good friends Jeff and Janet Eisenbach over for dinner to meet me.

Jeff and Janet had lived on the island for 15 years and were practically natives. Both of them were strong Christians, and Janet was an avid hiker! She immediately volunteered to take me hiking on Kauai's famous Kalalau Trail on the Na Pali Coast—the very hike I had been dreaming about for months!

The next morning, Janet was at my door at eight thirty, ready to take me on my dream hike. The drive to the trail was breathtaking. Janet showed me the beach where local surfer Bethany Hamilton had lost her arm in a shark attack. Hamilton, who is a strong Christian, didn't give up on her surfing career and went on to make one of the greatest comebacks the surfing world has ever seen. Her story was later featured in the movie *Soul Surfer*, starring Dennis Quaid, whom I was privileged to interview on a second trip to Hawaii in 2010 during the making of the film.

The Kalalau Trail was steep and rugged, but the view along it was out of this world. Remember the movie *Jurassic Park*? The Kalalau Trail is where it was shot, probably because the beauty is so wild and prehistoric looking. Janet and I hiked about three miles on the narrow trail that hugged the cliff and looked out over the expanse of blue ocean.

Then we took a left turn that took us away from the coast and deeper into the mountain. The scenery changed drastically. We were now hiking in the forest with little direct sunlight—the tall bamboo trees grew together and squealed when the wind hit them. We crossed a small river and went inland for several miles.

Finally, the payoff. We heard it before we saw it—the famous Hanakapi'ai Falls. The 300-foot waterfall was as intimidating as it was beautiful. The spectacular falls created an inviting pool, and Janet and I couldn't wait to jump in. So in we went! The water was icy cold but so refreshing. Not bad for my first day in Hawaii. *Lord, You are showing off! And I am loving it! Please don't stop.* God didn't.

After our swim, we ate our power bars and got ready to head back. We had not brought enough water with us, and it was hot. We had only a few drops left between us when God blessed us again. Janet and I spotted a tree that had a fruit I had never seen before. It looked like a small red apple but tasted like a pear. But most importantly, it was juicy! It provided not only moisture but much-needed sugar. Janet told me that the fruit is known locally as a mountain apple. I was grateful. Again, I saw how God was going before us and providing for every detail. *If God can do all this,* I thought, *how much more can He bring the right man across my path at exactly the right time? Is anything too hard for God?*

The next two weeks flew by. Janet proved to be the best tour guide and friend I could have imagined. I reflected on God's goodness and how He had provided something I hadn't asked for but knew I would need: a companion. And not just any companion, but a Spirit-filled Christian woman who loved to hike and show off her island! She took me to "top secret" waterfalls that tourists had not yet discovered. We ate fresh ahi tuna almost every day (I love fish and could seriously eat it every day), and she introduced me to acai—the Brazilian berry known for its high antioxidant levels (higher than blueberries) that is a staple in Brazil and tastes great with banana in a smoothie.

I saw a rainbow almost every day that I was on Kauai—a reminder to me of God's many promises and also of the fact that I was in paradise, or as close to paradise as one can find on earth. *Lord,* I prayed, *thank You seems like such a small thing to say, but this trip was one of the most special times of my life. Thank You, Father, from the bottom of my heart.*

God's Love Is Extravagant

My Hawaii adventure was so supernatural—yet it was so natural. Our heavenly Father is an extravagant God. *His love is extravagant.*

Like the dad I mentioned in an earlier chapter who took each of his daughters on her first date and set a high standard for her of how a man should treat her, when God does something, He does it first class and all the way. When He says, "I'm going to take care of things," He means it.

The Word of God says,

> For your Maker is your husband, the LORD of hosts is His name; and your Redeemer is the Holy One of Israel; He is called the God of the whole earth. For the LORD has called you like a woman forsaken and grieved in spirit, like a youthful wife when you were refused," says your God (Isa. 54:5-6).

I'm praying for an earthly husband, but in the meantime, my heavenly husband showed me how I should be treated and took me on an all-expenses-paid trip to Hawaii!

The Scripture the Lord gave me for this trip, Revelation 7:17, was part of a song that someone had given me before I left: "I will lead you to springs of living water; I will shepherd you." The passage itself says, "The Lamb who is in the midst of the throne will shepherd them and lead them to living fountains of waters. And God will wipe away every tear from their eyes." God spoke to me over and over throughout my trip of His tender and amazing love for me.

Jesus expressed God's abundant love toward us this way: "If anyone thirsts, let him come to Me and drink. He who believes in Me, as the Scripture has said, out of his heart will flow rivers of living water" (John 7:37-38). And in the Old Testament, we read more of God's lavish love toward us: "For the LORD your God is bringing you into a good land of flowing streams and pools of water, with fountains and springs that gush out in the valleys and hills" (Deut. 8:7, *NLT*).

Hopefully, you're getting the message by now. God is an *extravagant* God. Not only did He create a paradise like Hawaii for us to enjoy, but His love for us cannot be measured (see Eph 3:14-21). He longs to take us on adventures with Him, to lead us to springs of living waters, to refresh our tired body, soul and spirit.

He will do exceedingly abundantly more than we can dream or imagine. He's not a stingy God—He's generous. And guess what? He owns it all. I could have bought my own plane ticket, but God, being the generous and extravagant God that He is, bought it for me, because He wanted me to feel special and taken care of. A good husband takes care of those kinds of things for us.

Ladies, I believe the Lord is saying this to you:

Daughter, I love you very much; you are precious in My sight. I will give you the desires of your heart if you will only believe. Believe that I want to bless you. Believe that I'm for you, not against you. Believe that you are special to Me. I know the number of hairs on your head; I am a God of details. I'm in the details—those details that are so important to women. I want to give you a new heart—a heart that can believe Me for the impossible. Is anything too hard for Me? Just believe.

First John 3:1 says, "See what great love the Father has *lavished* on us, that we should be called children of God! And that is what we are!" (*NIV*, emphasis added). You are God's precious daughter, and God wants to *lavish* His love upon you. He wants to lead you to His refreshing springs of living waters and give you hope—hope for a glorious future. He will do exceedingly, abundantly greater things than we can dream or imagine.

Walk of Faith

Waiting on God to arrange this trip for me was a walk of faith. It was hard for me to believe at times that it would actually happen, and I even cried a few tears in moments of uncertainty, especially in those months when I heard nothing from the Lord. *Was God really going to do what He had said He would? Would He make a way for me?*

But I held on in faith, and God was faithful. He did everything He had said He would do and much more. He only asked one thing of me: *Will you believe me, daughter?*

What about you? What are you believing God for? Are you believing God for a mate? I am. If God can take me on an all-expenses-paid trip to Hawaii, how much more can He provide the perfect companion for my life—and for yours? Will He not do all that He has promised and more if we simply believe? As Jesus once told a man in serious need, "All things are possible to him who believes" (Mark 9:23).

God cares about the things we care about. He cares about the details of our lives and the desires of our hearts. And while He's working, He wants us to rest in Him. Maybe even take a vacation. As we step out in faith, trusting Him with our lives and our deep desires, He will refresh our hearts.

Prayer

Father, help us to believe You for big things! To have big dreams! Whether it's an extravagant, much-needed vacation, a new home or a wonderful husband to share our lives with. Lord, You promise us that if we delight ourselves in You, You will give us the desires of our hearts [see Ps. 37:4]. Father, help us to realize the vast resources that are at our disposal as daughters of the Most High King—and the vast favor that each of us has in You. You are able. You are faithful. Your love is extravagant! We will believe Your promises, and You will do the rest. In Jesus' name, amen.

REFLECTIONS

1. Has God ever given you an instruction similar to "Pack your bags, and I'll do the rest?"
2. What happened when you obeyed God?
3. What can we learn from Wendy's story and how she took God at His word?

WENDY GRIFFITH

21

MAKE ROOM FOR THE BLESSINGS OF GOD

Then he said, "About this time next year you shall embrace a son."
2 KINGS 4:16

Not too long ago I decided it was time to throw away some flowers that I'd had in a vase in my kitchen for two years! They were fairly dead, as you can imagine, but when I had first received them, they had been the most beautiful multi-colored baby roses that I had ever been given.

When they died, they kept their color and looked pretty, so I kept them in a vase on my kitchen coffee table. But now I noticed that they had lost all their color, and their dead, dried leaves were scattered all over my kitchen floor, making a huge mess. A guy I was seeing at the time was coming to visit in a couple days, so I was cleaning the house, and I decided it was time to throw away those once beautiful but now decidedly dead roses. So I swept the floor, threw out the flowers and put the vase back in the cupboard.

Well, about two days later, I went to the airport to pick up my guy friend who had flown in from Pittsburgh, and guess what he was holding in his hands? Tulips—beautiful multi-colored tulips, similar to the roses (when they had been alive) that I'd thrown away two days earlier. I immediately felt as if the Lord was teaching me something important: *Wendy, when you get rid of dead, old, dusty, tired things in your life, I will bring you something new, something fresh and something very much alive.*

This made me think of my closet. If you're like me, you tend to hold onto clothes long after you've stopped wearing them. The garments may not even fit, if you've lost or gained weight, or perhaps they're simply not in style anymore. I had lots of jackets and shirts with shoulder pads, which were particularly fashionable in the 90s— not so much today. However, I found that when I finally started to part with some of my fashion faux pas and oldies but goodies, I began to notice a pattern. Often someone would bless me with a new piece of clothing or I would end up finding exactly what I was looking for at the store. Every time I filled a plastic garbage bag with clothes and took it to the church or to the Salvation Army, God blessed me with something new to wear.

The wardrobe stylist at CBN, Sherry Wade, would call me and say, "Wendy, I've got some new dresses for you to try on." Or my mother would send me a new sweater out of the blue. It's the same principle I learned with the dead flowers: When *we* make room, God can bring us something new. He can bring a blessing, but first we have to throw some things away.

The principle of making room for God is well illustrated in the biblical story of the Shunammite woman from 2 Kings 4. The Shunammite woman *literally* made room for God, and it changed her life dramatically:

> Now it happened one day that Elisha went to Shunem, where there was a notable woman, and she persuaded him to eat some food. So it was, as often as he passed by, he would turn in there to eat some food. And she said to her husband, "Look now, I know that this is a holy man of God,

who passes by us regularly. Please, let us make a small upper room on the wall; and let us put a bed for him there, and a table and a chair and a lampstand; so it will be, whenever he comes to us, he can turn in there."

And it happened one day that he came there, and he turned in to the upper room and lay down there. Then he said to Gehazi his servant, "Call this Shunammite woman." When he had called her, she stood before him. And he said to him, "Say now to her, 'Look, you have been concerned for us with all this care. What can I do for you? Do you want me to speak on your behalf to the king or to the commander of the army?'"

She answered, "I dwell among my own people."

So he said, "What then is to be done for her?"

And Gehazi answered, "Actually, she has no son, and her husband is old."

So he said, "Call her." When he had called her, she stood in the doorway. Then he said, "About this time next year you shall embrace a son."

And she said, "No, my lord. Man of God, do not lie to your maidservant!"

But the woman conceived, and bore a son when the appointed time had come, of which Elisha had told her (4:8-17).

After the Shunammite had carefully built a room for Elisha the prophet in her home so that he would have a place to rest along his journeys, Elisha wanted to know, "What can I do for you? You've gone to all this trouble for me; now what can I do for you?" He practically begged the woman for a response.

But she answered, "I dwell among my own people." In other words, she was pretty comfortable. She already had all the political connections she needed with the king and the army, and she was wealthy. But God was determined to bless her. Notice that Elisha called his servant again and said, "There must be something we can do for her."

When Gehazi brought up the fact that the woman didn't have a son, Elisha called her again and said to her, "About this time next year you will have a son."

I love the Shunammite woman's response: "No, my lord, do not lie to your maidservant!" In other words, she was saying, "Do not make me believe again for the thing I believed for a long time ago but that never came to pass. I can't take any more disappointment." Elijah had apparently hit on something close to her heart—so close, in fact, that she had buried it where no one could see the desire anymore, not even her. But God saw it, and He wanted to do something about it.

You see, when we make room for God, we give Him, the Almighty, the Maker of heaven and Earth, permission to bless us. He will bring new life to old dreams. He will resurrect that dream that you thought was dead, that hope that you thought was buried, and He will give you the deep desires of your heart, even when you have lost the ability to ask for them as the Shunammite woman had.

Have you ever heard God whisper that question deep down in your spirit? *What can I, your heavenly Father, do for you, my daughter?* When we make room for God, He looks for ways to bless us, because our faith touches the very heart of God. And of course, we can never out-give the Lord.

My Dream to Anchor the News

God spoke particularly to me through this Scripture back in the spring of 2000. I had been at the Christian Broadcasting Network for about a year and a half, working in our Washington DC office, where I was the Capitol Hill correspondent. I was there the year of President Bill Clinton's impeachment trial. Talk about sink or swim—the impeachment story was one of the biggest of the last century and my first on-air assignment with CBN. I wanted to impress, but I also wanted to survive one of the darkest years in Washington DC's history. The spiritual gloom that covered our nation's capital was so thick that you could have cut it with a knife. Being on the Hill was a great experience, but I was thrilled and a bit relieved to be called down to CBN's headquarters in Virginia Beach the year after the Clinton story.

Although my background was both anchoring and reporting, at this point I was only reporting at CBN. I was interested in working as an anchor, but it didn't look as if there would be any opportunities for me to do so in the foreseen future. The anchors CBN had were all pretty established in their jobs.

But one night in May of 2000, as I was down on my knees praying, I heard the Lord tell me that I would anchor the news on the *700 Club*. It was a crazy feeling, as if God had just dropped a bomb into my spirit. I was excited and scared at the same time, and my reaction was much like the Shunammite woman's: "No, my Lord, don't lie to your maidservant." I was still on my knees, and tears streamed down my face.

Maybe my desire to be an anchor was a greater one than I had realized. I had told myself that I was content being only a reporter. It was challenging and fun, and I got to travel internationally for CBN doing interviews and stories. I reported on major happenings all over the world—not merely local news on boring city council meetings and trailer fires. *How could anything be missing in my life?* I asked.

I loved CBN. I was grateful to be able to report the news from a Christian perspective and to work in a place where I could pray with someone in the hallway and no one would think anything of it—in fact, someone might even stop to join in. Still, God saw what I was refusing to see—that I still wanted to be an anchor! I prayed, *Lord, if this is You, please speak to me.* I opened my Bible, and it opened to this very Scripture: "About this time next year you will hold a son in your arms."

I knew that God was not speaking to me about a literal son but that He was saying, *About this time next year, you will be on the anchor desk for the* 700 Club.

And so it was. On May 17, 2001, almost exactly one year later, I anchored the news for the first time on the *700 Club.*

See, anchoring the news was a dream that I had let die, but God, who searches the heart and knows our deep desires, brought it back to life. Like the Shunammite woman, I had made room for God when I had dedicated my life to Christ years earlier, and again when I later dedicated my career to Him. Because of that, I believe the Lord took me from broadcasting to an audience of 37 counties in my home state of West Virginia to one of 200-plus countries all over the world.

My Dream to Be Married

Even after all these years of singleness, I still have a dream to be married to a wonderful godly man. The dream is still very much alive, although (like you, I imagine) I have good days and bad days—days of great faith and days of not-so-great faith. But I've been given too many promises from God to give up now (I'll share some of those in chapter 23). But some of you have been believing God for a husband for so long that you're like the Shunammite woman: You've buried that desire and told yourself, *Well, I guess it's never going to happen; I guess singleness is my lot in life. I'm not going to believe for that anymore.*

Friend, not only has God not forgotten you, but I believe He's remembering you right now, just as He remembered the Shunammite woman. In fact, your name is written on the palm of His hand: "See, I have inscribed you on the palms of My hands; your walls are continually before Me" (Isa. 49:16). He thinks about you constantly and wants to bless you more than you want to be blessed.

The secret, I believe, to the Shunammite woman's fulfilled desire is that she put God first. The Bible says, "Seek first the kingdom of God and His righteousness, and all these [other] things [that you desire—like a husband] shall be added to you" (Matt. 6:33).

When the Shunammite woman urged her husband, saying, "Let's make a room for this man of God," she was getting her priorities in order. Maybe she really wanted to redo the carpet in her house or buy some new furniture for the living room, but instead she made a room for the man of God so that when he passed through her village, he could rest and put his feet up and maybe enjoy a home-cooked meal. In a sense, this woman put God first, and He in turn put her first. "Take delight in the LORD, and he will give you the desires of your heart" (Ps. 37:4, *NIV*).

Miracles Happen

When we make room for God, God will even do miracles for us. What happened to the Shunammite woman was no less than a miracle. The Scripture says that her husband was old. That means that in the natural, his body may have been too old to help her conceive a son—but not too old for God to help him out. God gave this couple the ability to conceive a baby. He did a miracle, whether in the husband or in the wife, and the Shunammite woman conceived and bore a son at exactly the time that the prophet had said she would.

Why did God do that for her? She had been relatively content. There were probably lots of people who envied her social standing and lifestyle. But God looked into her heart and saw the deep longing that was still there: the craving to hold a baby in her arms, to snuggle him, to hold him to her chest and breastfeed, to bathe and feed him. She had never had these experiences that so many of the other women in her village had had. Now God, in His infinite mercy, was going to grant her that deep yet hidden desire. *That's the heart of God for you too, daughter.* And when the Shunammite woman blessed the man of God—well, you might say that God was, in a way, obligated to bless her. It's His nature; it's the law of reciprocity; it's the law of sowing and reaping. Ladies, we can't out-give God! He wants to bless our socks off. He wants to give us the deep desires of our heart.

But so often it seems that God is waiting on us to make the first move. For the Shunammite woman, it meant building a room for the man of God.

What does it mean for you? How can you make room for the blessings of God? I know that for me personally, I could spend more time with Him. Like many of you, I sometimes struggle to find five minutes to pray, let alone an hour, but I know that when I make the time to sit at the Lord's feet, to read His Word, to worship Him and to pray, I'm the one who is blessed. It is time well spent.

I'm a firm believer that the principle of making room for the new works. It was as if God was waiting on me to throw those ugly dead flowers away so He could bring me new ones. And there I was hanging onto those dead flowers month after month after month. Why? I think I simply got used to them. So often we hold onto the past. We hold onto something that has no life left in it, whether it's a vase of old flowers or a relationship that God has declared d-e-a-d, over and done, and we unknowingly forsake or delay the blessing that is waiting.

I don't want to delay my blessings. I remember that after my breakup with Michael, the Lord said to me, *If you don't go back but instead keep going forward, you will be blessed.*

God says, "Do not remember the former things, nor consider the things of old. Behold, I will do a new thing, now it shall spring forth; shall you not know it?" (Isa. 43:19).

Make room for God. He is waiting to pour out a blessing on you.

Prayer

Father, help us to make room for You! And not only in our closets but in our hearts. Help us to get rid of the old—old flowers, old mindsets and old relationships, if necessary. You have so much more for us. Lord, give us the desire of our hearts as we put You first. And help us to make room for the incredible blessings, including a wonderful godly husband, that You have stored up for us. In Jesus' name, amen.

REFLECTIONS

1. What are some things you need to get rid of in order to make room for God's blessings in your life?
2. Are you holding onto dead things that have no life left in them? What are some examples of dead things?
3. How can we make room in our hearts for the one God has for us?

22

BE THE PRIZE!

He who finds a wife finds a good thing.
PROVERBS 18:22

Our inner beauty is more important and more lasting than any other kind of beauty. But that doesn't mean that we are to pay no attention to our outer beauty.

Our body is a gift from God. It's the temple of the Holy Spirit. The Bible says that we are to honor God with our bodies:

> Do you not know that your bodies are temples of the Holy Spirit, who is in you, whom you have received from God? You are not your own; you were bought at a price. Therefore honor God with your bodies (1 Cor. 6:19-20, *NIV*).

Honor God with Your Bodies

What does this mean?

I think it means that Christians should be the healthiest, most in-shape people on the planet. We should set the example when it comes to having healthy bodies. Okay, even as I write this, I'm feeling a little convicted. I love chocolate and eat it almost every day—dark chocolate mostly. But, fortunately, I also enjoy eating healthy foods and working out, so that balances out my chocolate intake. But many Christians simply don't understand the vital importance of taking care of their bodies.

First of all, our health is our greatest physical asset. We can't put a price tag on our health—it's priceless. If we're going to do great exploits for God, then we need all our strength. And if we're going to attract a mate who is in good shape, then should we not be in good shape as well? It's only fair, right?

I had a girlfriend who was a bit overweight, but she was attracted to muscular, in-shape guys. I felt terrible for her because none of the guys she talked to me about ever asked her out on a date. My friend didn't understand, but it's pretty simple: Just as she was, those men were attracted to members of the opposite sex who took care of their bodies.

If you want a Superman, than you'd better do your best to look and act like Lois Lane: smart, sexy and confident.

Men, including Christian men, are visual creatures. They're attracted to beauty and femininity as well as to a woman's inner qualities and strengths.

Yes, we're all striving to be the Proverbs 31 woman, whom the Bible says is strong, virtuous, dignified, wise, godly and talented. But what almost always attracts a man first is the way we look and the way we carry ourselves. Are you confident when you walk into a room, or do you hold your head down as if you're embarrassed that someone might see you? Do you make eye contact with the opposite sex or look away before there's any chance of having a conversation?

What Are Men Looking For?

One Sunday after church, I was having coffee with my friend Hanisha at a local Starbucks. As we sipped our ice coffees under the umbrella at an outdoor table, we struck up a conversation with a couple of Christian guys who were sitting at the table next to us. In the name of "research," I asked them to be honest and to tell me what attracted them to a woman—what first caught their eye about someone of the opposite sex.

Eric, a dark-haired, attractive 36-year-old single Christian man from Florida who had an M.B.A., told me, "It's the smile and the eyes for me. A smile tells you so much about a woman; it really gives you a glimpse of her outlook on life. Also, I like a bubbly personality. If I'm going to spend the rest of my life with someone, I don't want her to be a bump on a log. I'm also attracted to brunettes and to outdoorsy, athletic types—women I could see myself hiking or camping with."

His friend Aaron, a 32-year-old attorney from Virginia, was more to the point: "Good face, good legs, intelligent and thoughtful. I like a woman who is aware and caring of other people. It's a big turn-off, even if she's beautiful, if she thinks she's the only person alive."

Eric and Aaron confirmed that just as women are, men are looking for the whole package. Attractive, godly, humorous—someone with whom they can see themselves spending a lifetime. And ladies, let me assure you. You already have all the right equipment; you may simply need a little fine-tuning. And frankly, who doesn't?

Let me ask you: Are you working out? Are you keeping your body healthy and toned? As I said before, your health is your number one physical asset and is a gift from God; guard it jealously. Make time in your schedule to work out and to eat well.

This is not vanity; it's common sense, and it's obedience to God's command to honor our bodies. I love to exercise not only for the physical benefits but for the mental and emotional benefits as well. I love how I feel after 20 minutes on the stair climber (my favorite machine at the gym). I try to use the stair climber three times a week and to walk for about 45 minutes on the other days. I also do push-ups, sit-ups and squats daily. The more fit I am, the more confident I feel when I'm standing at the anchor desk reading the news, conducting an interview or going on a date.

As actor Henry Cavill, the star of the movie *Man of Steel*, told me during an interview, he endured grueling workouts to prepare to play the role of Superman. He told *Muscle & Fitness* magazine there was a time in one of his workouts in which he had to push the limits of what he thought was physically possible for him. It was then that he had a breakthrough moment, and he actually felt as if he had earned the role and the right to play Superman. Well, you and I might not be vying for the role of Superman, but we are the leading ladies in the most important stories on earth: our own lives! And guess what? There are no dress rehearsals. We get one chance, baby! One chance to be our best, look our best and feel our best.

Why not go for it? Do it for you! You are a prize to be won! Be the prize.

Be the prize for yourself first—and then watch what happens. You'll be surprised at how taking care of you will give you extra confidence and bounce in your step.

My sister, Nancy St. John, is a perfect example of the fact that fitness equals confidence. Nancy is a gorgeous long-legged blonde in her early 40s with loads of confidence. But she wasn't always that way. She struggled with her weight for years and always felt that something was missing from her life or that she wasn't the person she wanted to be. Then, to use her words, she became "passionate about exercise"! Nancy began running, taking spin classes and lifting weights to get in shape and then to maintain her weight and her figure.

Nancy liked staying in shape so much that she decided to help others with their fitness goals! She now teaches aerobics and spin classes, which combine cardio, weights and sculpting exercises. She still runs and walks several times a week.

Nancy's advice? "Exercise makes me feel great and is the one thing I can always count on to put me in a great mood"—but she cautions that exercise alone is not enough to maintain an ideal weight: "Exercise is only about 10 to 20 percent responsible for how you look; diet is about 80 to 90 percent responsible and, of course, your genetics will play a role also. I finally got the results I wanted after I stopped eating bread and sugar, although I still eat pizza about once a month." Nancy warns women not to compare themselves to the airbrushed beauties in the grocery-store magazines: "You have to make sure your goal is to be healthy, not to try to look like a supermodel. If you are as healthy as you can be, you will look as good as you can look, and you will feel as good as you can feel!"

Nancy's words make me want to go for a hike right now!

You Are What You Speak

In his inspiring book *It's Your Time*, Joel Osteen talks about the importance of faith-filled words and how we need to be careful about what we speak to ourselves. The Bible says, "We will have the fruit of our lips"—in other words, we will have what we say. Osteen recounts the story of a staff member from Lakewood Church in Houston who once confessed to him that before she left the house every morning, she looked in the mirror and said, "Girl, you are looking good today!" Osteen says,

> Shouldn't we be our own best friends and cheerleaders? Yet most of the time, we put ourselves down worse than we would an enemy: "I don't look good today. I'm overweight, I'm unattractive. I can't do anything right." Don't speak defeat over your life. Your words prophesy what you become. Be bold. Dare to say, "I look great today. I'm made in the image of Almighty God. I am strong and talented. . . ." Our words truly do have creative power. If you want to know what you will be like five years from now, just listen to what you say today.

The Bible says that we are "fearfully and wonderfully made" (Ps. 139:14). When I'm feeling down about the way I look, I repeat this Scripture over and over until I believe it. "I am fearfully and wonderfully made!" God doesn't make mistakes. Maybe you think your nose is too big or your thighs are too fat. I happen to think big noses give a face character! A cute little pug nose is fine too, but if you've got a big nose, embrace it. Barbara Streisand did; so did Sarah Jessica Parker—and she's one of the faces of Revlon! Although Parker does not have the typical Hollywood beauty look, she's got something even better, in my opinion: confidence. Loads and loads of confidence! And that truly makes her beautiful.

Remember Jennifer Grey, who played the role of Baby in the popular '80s movie *Dirty Dancing*? She had an interesting nose—it had a little hump in it, but it gave her face character. After the movie, she got a nose job, and the result was a pretty but generic-looking nose. It changed her face and her look so much that people couldn't even recognize her from the movie. She blames her nose job for adversely affecting her career: "I went into the operating room a celebrity and came out anonymous," she said. "It was the nose job from hell. I'll always be this once-famous actress nobody recognizes because of a nose job."[1]

The painful lesson she learned was that she should have embraced what she had. Her look made her unique—it made her Jennifer Grey. Now of course there are exceptions—perhaps getting a nose job was the best decision you ever made, and it actually improved your life and gave you tons more confidence. Or maybe you needed a nose job for health reasons to help you breath better. Deciding to do something as drastic as plastic surgery is definitely a personal choice and worthy of much prayer.

Embrace What You've Got

The moral to the story: Embrace what God has given you, and make the most of it. Play up your best features. Do you have great hair? Beautiful eyes? Luscious lips? Great skin? A great figure? Accentuate the positive.

And remember, nobody is perfect. We all have areas we'd like to improve. But the truth is, it's often our imperfections that make us more interesting and even more beautiful. Can you imagine Cindy

Crawford without her mole—or rather, her beauty mark—on her face? No way. Loving yourself is healthy—with or without a relationship.

If you're not in a relationship right now, that's no excuse to let yourself go. In fact, this is the time to really take care of yourself. You never know when you'll bump into "the one." Plus, you have more time to focus on you right now. I love to get a manicure and a pedicure. I love feeling "finished" from head to toe.

Esther, in the Bible, certainly did not ignore beauty treatments before she went in to see the king:

> Each young woman's turn came to go in to King Ahasuer-us after she had completed twelve months' preparation, according to the regulations for the women, for thus were the days of their preparation apportioned: six months with oil of myrrh, and six months with perfumes and preparations for beautifying women (Esther 2:12).

Even Esther, as beautiful as she was, needed a little help. You're not being vain if you take time to get a facial or a manicure or put getting to the gym as a priority on your weekly to-do list. Your body and your beauty are gifts from God. Nurture your body, take care of it, be kind to it—and it will be kind to you.

Enjoy you! You are one of a kind. My sisters both have cute feet and toes, while I have large feet and long, slightly crooked toes—thanks, Dad! But I also got my dad's long, graceful fingers. We can't have everything! But we can certainly make the most of what we do have. When I get a pedicure, my feet look great, even with my long toes! Not as great as my sisters', but still pretty good.

The Camera Doesn't Lie

I like to feel strong and in shape, but I also like fitting into my clothes. Besides that, the camera doesn't lie. Every day that I'm on television, the camera tells me if I'm enjoying too many French fries or too much ice cream. Yes, I do eat carbs! But if I have fries, I usually only have a few. And I do love ice cream—in fact, after my breakup, Ben and Jerry's Chunky Monkey became my favorite indulgence. But once I noticed that my dresses were fitting a little too tightly, I put the ice cream away—as hard as it was to do it! I still indulge from time to time, of course. After all, great food is one of life's great pleasures. But nothing tastes as good as looking good feels.

The Power of a Dress

I have discovered something that I am sure many women throughout the ages realized long before I did: There seems to be some magical power in wearing a dress. For years I wore black pants and a blouse or camisole with a blazer. It was almost like a uniform. And it worked well for a season in my life. But several years ago, I noticed that on the days I wore a dress, especially a particularly feminine-looking dress, I would get a lot more attention from the opposite sex. Guys I worked with would say, "Wow! You look great!" or, "That's a great dress." It was uncanny. I couldn't get over the reactions.

I asked one of my female colleagues who wore a dress every day and who always looked polished if she got the same reactions. "Yes!" she said. "It does make a difference, not only in how you feel and carry yourself, but in how others treat you as well. Plus, it makes getting up at four o'clock a little easier," she said.

Trust me, there's something about a dress paired with a good pair of heels that says, "I'm a woman." We only have one life to live—there's no dress rehearsal. So why not wear a dress, why not hit the gym and break a sweat, why not go for that hike and why not eat that healthy meal you've been telling yourself you are going to start eating? (And if you really want to glow, check out the recipe for my healthy green drink in the back of the book.) You'll be glad you did these things, and the people around you will notice the unmistakable glow when you walk in a room.

Be the prize that you were born to be!

Prayer

Dear heavenly Father, thank You for the gift of our bodies. Help us to take care of our bodies, to nurture them and to be kind to them. Help us to remember that we are fearfully and wonderfully made and that You knit us together in our mothers' wombs. Lord, we desire to be strong, healthy and beautiful for You. Give us wisdom. Help Your daughters, as You helped Queen Esther, to be ready for our "moment"—and may it be "for such a time as this" [Esther 4:14]. In Jesus' name, amen.

REFLECTIONS

1. What are some things that you know you need to do in order to be ready to date or to get married?
2. Why is it important to be the kind of person you want to date?
3. Why is it important to enjoy and to celebrate your time of singleness?

23

GOD'S PROMISES

Search from the book of the LORD, *and read:*
Not one of these shall fail; not one shall lack her mate.
For My mouth has commanded it, and His Spirit has gathered them.
ISAIAH 34:16

It was mid-January 2009, and CBN was in the midst of our biggest fundraising drive of the year: our annual two-week-long winter Telethon. I love our Telethons, as they seem to bring our entire staff together and allow us to interact with each other in a way that we normally don't. Telethon time is also a reminder that without God's provision, we can do nothing. During Telethon, our unity is more pronounced, our prayers are more earnest and focused, and our victories are more supernatural.

It's a great time for the ministry, to be sure, but on this particular Telethon Day, I was asking the Lord about something personal: my future husband. "Lord," I prayed, "You see me serving You day after day, week after week, year after year, and it's a great privilege to do it. I'm so happy to have this opportunity to do what You've called me to do and to help advance your kingdom here on Earth. Nothing could be greater! But I sure would like to know if you have a husband for me, because I would really like one."

I had my Bible with me on the set, and during breaks between my on-air times, I opened the Scriptures. On one of my breaks my Bible fell open at Ruth chapter 3. My eyes locked onto verse 1:

One day, Naomi said to Ruth: It's time I found you a husband, who will give you a home and take care of you (*CEV*).

The *NIV* says it like this: "One day Ruth's mother-in-law Naomi said to her, 'My daughter, I must find a home for you, where you will be well provided for.'" And the *New King James Version* uses the word "security" instead of "husband": "My daughter, shall I not seek security for you, that it may be well with you?" This is interesting, because studies show that security (both emotional and financial) is the number one thing most women desire in a marriage relationship.

Naomi's sage advice to Ruth continues in verses 2-5:

"Now Boaz, whose young women you were with, is he not our relative? In fact, he is winnowing barley tonight at the threshing floor. Therefore wash yourself and anoint yourself, put on your best garment and go down to the threshing floor; but do not make yourself known to the man until he has finished eating and drinking. Then it shall be, when he lies down, that you shall notice the place where he lies; and you shall go in, uncover his feet, and lie down; and he will tell you what you should do."

And she said to her, "All that you say to me I will do."

I was more than pleased that the Lord seemed to answer my prayer with such a specific Scripture. I love it when the Lord so graciously speaks to us through His Word. I tucked that word away in my heart and did not mention it to anyone. It was time to go back on the air. Pete, the floor director, gave me the standby: "Coming to you, Wendy, in 3 . . . 2 . . . I smiled and pitched the premium (usually a powerful biblical teaching by Pat or Gordon Robertson on DVD), something we give away as an incentive and an encouragement for people to join the *700 Club*.

That evening, after a busy day at work, I was driving home from CBN, taking my usual scenic route in order to avoid highway traffic, when my eye caught the vanity plate on the car in front of me. I couldn't believe my eyes. It read, "RUTH31."

Even now, more than four years later, tears come to my eyes as I remember God's faithfulness and how He so lovingly speaks to us, not only through His Word, which is alive and powerful and sharper than a two-edged sword, but even through vanity plates! Only God knew that I had earlier in the day, after a heartfelt prayer about my future husband, turned to Ruth 3:1, and now He was confirming His word to me through this innocent driver—who will never know how much her being in the right place at the right time blessed me.

The Bible says, "By the mouth of two or three witnesses every word shall be established" (2 Cor. 13:1). Seeing that Scripture reference was all the confirmation I needed. Four years later, that promise is still as fresh to me as the day God gave it. Although I haven't met my prince yet, that promise to me is as good as gold. All I have to do is wait on God's perfect timing. Easier said than done, of course, but when we know that we have a promise from God, we know that He's going to fulfill it.

Don't Birth an Ishmael

Ishmael was Abraham's first son, born by his marriage to Sarah's handmaiden Hagar. But Ishmael was not the promised son:

> Now Sarai, Abram's wife, had borne him no children. But she had an Egyptian slave named Hagar; so she said to Abram, "The LORD has kept me from having children. Go, sleep with my slave; perhaps I can build a family through her."

Abram agreed to what Sarai said. So after Abram had been living in Canaan ten years, Sarai his wife took her Egyptian slave Hagar and gave her to her husband to be his wife. He slept with Hagar, and she conceived. . . .

The angel of the LORD . . . said to [Hagar]:

"You are now pregnant and you will give birth to a son. You shall name him Ishmael, for the LORD has heard of your misery.

He will be a wild donkey of a man; his hand will be against everyone and everyone's hand against him, and he will live in hostility toward all his brothers. . . ."

Abram was eighty-six years old when Hagar bore him Ishmael (Gen. 16:1-4, 11-12, 16, *NIV*, emphasis added).

God had promised Abraham that He would give him a son in his old age by his wife Sarah, but God did not tell Abraham how long he would have to wait for the child. As the long years passed and Abraham and Sarah continued to get older, they decided to help God out. They took matters into their own hands, so to speak. You know what happened—Ishmael happened.

Now it wasn't that God didn't love Ishmael. He did! And He made him into a great nation. But Ishmael wasn't "the one"—he wasn't the son that God had promised Abraham—and the result of Abraham and Sarah not waiting on God's perfect timing was disastrous. In fact, the consequences of their actions are still being played out today in the Arab-Israeli conflict.

Don't birth an Ishmael—wait on God, even though it can be tough to do. Even Abraham, whom the Bible calls the father of faith (see Heb. 4:11), had a hard time believing that God could give him a son when he was nearly 100 years old (which is why he ended up fathering Ishmael):

Abraham fell facedown; he laughed and said to himself, "Will a son be born to a man a hundred years old? Will Sarah bear a child at the age of ninety?" And Abraham said to God, "If only Ishmael might live under your blessing!"

Then God said, "Yes, but your wife Sarah will bear you a son, and you will call him Isaac. I will establish my covenant with him as an everlasting covenant for his descendants after him. And as for Ishmael, I have heard you: I will surely bless him; I will make him fruitful and will greatly increase his numbers. He will be the father of twelve rulers, and I will make him into a great nation. But my covenant I will establish with Isaac, whom Sarah will bear to you by this time next year" (Gen. 17:17-21, *NIV*).

God's appointed times can be very hard for us to wait for, but they are always worth waiting for.

Put God First and Let Him Work Things Out

A good friend of mine, Jensine Bard, is one of the most vivacious, radiant, on-fire-for-Jesus women I know. Although she is extremely beautiful and talented, true love eluded her for many years. But God was faithful. Here's Jensine's story:

> I knew what I wanted to be when I was three. Standing in my undies on my grandfather's porch, wearing a big black hat, I announced, "I'm goin' to Hollywood and be a movie star!" Years later, that would happen—at least to some degree!
>
> I began traveling and touring as a professional singer at age 17, right out of high school, with a pianist from Europe. I would eventually go on to form my own band, tour with other groups, showcase in Las Vegas, and finally wind up in Palm Springs at the invitation of an uncle who was an aspiring opera singer and tennis pro. Soon after I arrived in Palm Springs, my uncle moved away, and I needed to find a way to support myself. Fortunately, I found work singing, modeling

and hostessing at local top spots. I even sang under contract for singing cowboy and Angels baseball owner Gene Autry.

When it came to men, I didn't have trouble getting a date or a boyfriend, but relationships never seemed to last. I would be drawn to the tall, dark and handsome types, but inside, these guys weren't so handsome, and things would always fizzle or end in a disappointing way. And, to be honest, my career was leaving me empty as well. I knew there had to be more.

It was during this time when I was in my early 20s that through a series of divine appointments and godly relationships I came to know the *real* saving, healing and delivering power of a Savior I so desperately needed. Soon everything began to change, including my view of men, which had been less than favorable!

In my newfound faith, Jesus was now Lord of my life and not just someone I made a once-a-week visit to in the local church pew. But now I wondered, still single at age 30-plus, *Where is His mate for me?!*

With this question swirling through my head, I sat at the kitchen table of my friend, mentor and mother in the Lord, Connie. Almost reading my thoughts, she suddenly announced, "You need to make a list of everything you want in a husband!"

"A list?" I said. Uh oh! *That means that whatever I put on that list, that's it!* I thought. *That's what I'll get.* I wasn't the fearful type, but for some reason, I really believed that whatever I put on that list would be it. No! So instead I offered this simple prayer, "Lord, make me the woman of God You want me to be. Send me the man of God You want me to have, and bring him in Your time."

How safe is that?!

But no, that wasn't going to cut it—I needed to be specific, Connie said! So for the first time, at my mentor's urging,

I began to write down everything that I wanted in a husband—and I mean everything! In two minutes, I had my list, and quite the impressive list it was! Who on earth could possibly fill all these requirements?

Several years later, *and still no husband.*

A few dates, yes! Good looking, yes! In the church, yes! A few outside the church, yes! The verdict? No match. Where was the towel? I was ready to throw it in!

At this point, I was thinking, *Love has to be simpler than this. A guy either is the right one or he isn't—and if you have to justify anything, then up go the red flags.* Or at least they should, and in my case they did! Let's see . . .

Mr. Paris, with his toupee and his *je t'aime*, wasn't "the one."

Mr. Full of Enthusiasm, who also needed me to ground him, wasn't "the one."

And Mr. Wonderful, successful but old enough to be my father, was surely not "the one"!

So who was? And where was he?

Meanwhile, I continued to live my life as fully as possible: I was a born-again, Spirit-filled Christian, singing on Christian television and in concert, leading worship, writing songs, evangelizing in the workplace, working for top CEOs and living with a Christian family that took me in to help me grow in my new and renewed life in Christ. "God sets the solitary in families" (Ps. 68:6).

We shared and sang about Jesus at dinner parties, and we did volunteer work, and I learned from my mentors and pastors valuable lessons in life and in the Lord—through tears, joy, down times and up times! There was no time for long faces, no "pity parties." Life was moving, and I was moving with it—to the point of exhaustion at times!

But where was God in my love life? (Still single at 38, and 15 years celibate—with the clock ticking!) *What was He waiting for?* What was I not doing, or what did I need to start doing?

I wrote songs of hope that helped heal my soul—songs about coming from the life I had known (the pits!) to my new life in Him (joy!). As I think back to those days, "Waiting" was the chapter I was certain to write, "Enduring" was the chapter I was certain to live, and "Expecting" was the chapter I needed to believe would be written in God's time, in God's way and with God's mate!

I reminded myself that it was about His choice for me— His highest and best! No settling, compromising, complaining or murmuring! I was His prize; was He my prize?

Absolutely—yes! "Love the Lord your God with all your heart, soul and mind" (see Luke 10:27). That was my goal, my passion and my purpose! So however God wanted to work out the rest was fine with me—my trust was in Him to give me the desires of my heart as I put Him first (see Ps. 37:4). "Seek first the kingdom of God and His righteousness, and all these things shall be added to you" (Matt. 6:33). I knew God would keep His promises!

Fast-forward several months.

The year was 1993. My spiritual parents, Connie and Bill McNally, were attending one of CBN's partner events in Virginia Beach, Virginia. Little did I know that the man who would become my future husband was also attending this conference. Dan Bard, a tall, handsome Midwestern businessman from Michigan with a great heart, was the answer to that list I had reluctantly but in obedience made *seven years earlier*!

During a Saturday morning service, Connie noticed the tall Midwesterner, his hands lifted high in worship, and boldly inquired of him, "Are you married?"

Stunned but intrigued, Dan answered, "No, I'm not."

Not one to miss an opportunity, Connie promptly and gleefully replied, "Well, have I got a girl for you."

Little did my friend Connie and her husband Bill know that only *five minutes* before Connie popped that question to

Dan, Dr. Pat Robertson, chairman and CEO of the Christian Broadcasting Network, had been asking another question of Dan and the men in the room: "Men, what do you want? Ask God for it!"

At that moment, Dan had responded silently, *God, I want a wife—a Proverbs 31 wife—beautiful inside and out.* Five minutes later, there was my mentor standing in front of Dan with a tape of my music, handing it to this man who would soon be my husband!

Back at the ranch—or, should I say, at the San Diego airport—Connie handed me Dan's business card with enthusiasm and said, "Have I got a guy for you!"

In the days that followed, I received a beautifully penned letter with a check along with a request to purchase one of my original musical recordings. (Dan had listened to the one given to him at CBN and loved it but had thoughtfully returned it to the McNallys before the conference ended.) It definitely seemed to have been a God-orchestrated meeting—but only time would tell.

We began a back-and-forth correspondence that included three-hour weekly phone calls (which seemed like 10 minutes)—and I did not even have a photo of this man I was falling in love with! He had one of me from the cover of my music tape, but I didn't have one of him. So I asked for one and finally received it—a pinkie nail-sized photo of him and his buddies up at his family cabin.

As I looked at a picture of this man I had gotten to know over the phone, I thought, *What?* But God was clearly showing me, ever so winsomely, that He had wanted me to know my future husband by the spirit *first* and *not* the flesh.

Still, I had an excitement and an anticipation—unlike with past relationships that had always seemed to fizzle and drop to the level of mediocrity! Not this time—and not for this girl! I wanted God's absolute highest and best, and I was willing to wait for it, come rain or shine, high water or drought—or simply not at all! If God had a mate for me, then He would bring it to pass. And with a little help from my friends, it seemed that *now* was that time!

THE MAN OF MY DREAMS (I HOPED!)

Dan and I decided that he would come out to California so that we could meet in person. I arranged for him to stay for three days at the Whispering Palms Golf Resort—right there on the green! He was a golfer, so this seemed the perfect place. His ticket was purchased, the date was set; he would fly out, we would meet, and we would see what God had in mind! A dinner at Delicias in Rancho Sante Fe with my mentor Connie and her husband Bill seemed like the perfect way to start things off.

I went to the resort to pick Dan up for dinner. After I parked the car, I hurried through the doors in excitement and anticipation, and I began to look for the man whose voice I had fallen in love with but whose face I had not seen— at least not in person anyway! As we approached one another, I heard myself say, "Dan?" and I heard him say in return, "Jensine?"

It was like a scene from a romantic movie. Finally—face to face—we met! But wait! Where were the bells?! And why weren't they ringing? (I later talked to a close married friend who told me that bells and whistles should not be the sole barometer you base your first, initial reaction on. Give it a chance—let it breathe, get to know him. That's advice I will always be grateful for!)

Dan and I ended up having a glorious time that night, and the days ahead would disprove any second thoughts or doubts that I had on our initial meeting. And why did I have them? Dan was tall, handsome, elegant. It seemed as though we had known each other forever, like we were hand in glove,

a natural fit. We just knew that God was bringing us together, to the point that if we didn't get married, it would be an
act of disobedience.

SATAN'S PLOY—THE COUNTERFEIT

How many of you know that when God begins to do a new
thing in your life, the enemy is there to try and stop it?
Two days before I first met my intended husband in person,
an old flame, "Mr. Paris," popped up out of nowhere in the
grocery store! Seeing him was further confirmation for me
that he was *not* the one for me—and it created greater anticipation for the one who *was*! Seeds of doubt were rejected; the
bait was not taken; and the counterfeit was exposed!

BACK TO THE STORY WITH DAN!

Dan's three days turned into an extended week of meeting
friends, going places, staying up for hours talking. It seemed
that everywhere we went, we were the only ones in the world,
whether we were walking the streets of La Jolla, Del Mar,
Rancho Santa Fe, Palm Desert. It felt as if one year was
packed into one week—supernaturally!

Then, halfway through the week, the list I had made
seven years earlier popped up out of nowhere in my makeup drawer! I had misplaced it and all but forgotten it, and
now here it was! As I began to read it, I was amazed to find
myself saying, "Check, check, check . . . This is it! This is
him!" He was everything on the list except for two things:
"sings beautifully" and "plays several different instru-
ments." Ha! Well, I told you that I put *everything* I could
think of on that list!

But here's how God answered even those two details.
Dan's last name is "Bard," a musical term, and he whistles
beautifully, which is something I cannot do! Of course, the
most important things on the list were that he would have

character and spiritual qualities, which Dan has in abundance—birthed, he will tell you, through the pain of overcoming, enduring and believing.

By halfway through Dan's visit, my attitude toward him had gone from "no bells" to "every bell in the church ringing" to *When is he going to ask me to marry him?!* I was not going to ask him! When a man really knows what he wants, he will initiate the process. We don't have to. That was my opinion at that time, and it still is today!

It was three in the afternoon at the Rancho Valencia Resort. There was no one there but Dan and I at a quaint table for two with a window view. We had stopped for a snack, and then, out of the blue, I heard, "Well, do you want to get married, or something like that?"

"Something like that"?! Yes, emphatically, yes! And the rest, as they say, is history!

By the end of the week, an engagement party had been planned. But now—where was the ring?

Earlier that week, at McNally Company Antiques in Rancho Santa Fe, we had been browsing, when a ring had caught the attention of my beloved. "Do you like that?" he had asked.

"Yes," I'd replied. This was, in fact, the same ring I had admired *six months earlier*. It was gold, vintage and unique. I had wanted it when I'd first seen it, but something had told me, "Wait"!

That is the ring Dan selected on the very night of our engagement party when he made a last-minute trip to that shop to surprise me. And what a surprise it was! The ring not only looked beautiful, but it fit perfectly!

Does God really want to give us the desires of our heart for a mate? More than we know! And will He make it plain and clear to us who our mate should be? Yes, if we allow Him to.

Dan and I were married November 27, 1993, in an intimate, black-tie, sterling silver, floral-laden evening wedding at the

You Are a Prize to Be Won!

fabulous Rancho Valencia Resort. Connie was my matron of honor, and her husband Bill walked me down the aisle. My spiritual family and my close friends, who had prayed and believed with me for my future husband, were now seeing the fruit of their prayers (and mine) answered! My pastor at the time, Peter Parris, who married us, prayed that God would use us "to strengthen the hands of the weak."

Our heart's desire together is just that: to be used by God to bless others as we have been blessed, whether through smooth sailing or rough waters. "What God has joined together, let no man put asunder," and with honor and commitment to our marriage," we hold fast the profession of our faith" and to each other!

Hallelujah!

All the miracles and confirmations that happened along the way are too much for me to expound upon here. Suffice it to say that when we let God choose our mate, when we are willing to wait and continue to "press toward the mark for the prize of the high calling of God in Christ Jesus" (Phil. 3:14, *KJV*) *during* the process, then *God* will bless us above and beyond all we can ask, think or imagine (see Eph. 3:20). He will heal your broken heart, deliver you and set you free, and set your feet on the path *He* has designed for you—perfectly and entirely!

Daughter, you will know *who* you are *in Christ*—a prize to be won—so that you can know in turn *who* Christ has for you! What God did for me, He will do for you. He will give unto you a gift that will be worth the wait![1]

Hannah's Promise from God

Another woman who never gave up but who believed God and received her promise from the Lord is Hannah. You're probably familiar with her story in the Bible. Hannah was married to a man named Elkanah who loved her very much. But he also had another wife named Peninnah. The Bible says,

Peninnah had children, but Hannah had no children. [Elkanah] went up from his city yearly to worship and sacrifice to the LORD of hosts in Shiloh. Also the two sons of Eli, Hophni and Phinehas, the priests of the LORD, were there. And whenever the time came for Elkanah to make an offering, he would give portions to Peninnah his wife and to all her sons and daughters. But to Hannah he would give a double portion, for he loved Hannah, although the LORD had closed her womb. And her rival also provoked her severely, to make her miserable, because the LORD had closed her womb. So it was, year by year, when she went up to the house of the LORD, that she provoked her; therefore she wept and did not eat.

Then Elkanah her husband said to her, "Hannah, why do you weep? Why do you not eat? And why is your heart grieved? Am I not better to you than ten sons?"

So Hannah arose after they had finished eating and drinking in Shiloh. Now Eli the priest was sitting on the seat by the doorpost of the tabernacle of the LORD. And she was in bitterness of soul, and prayed to the LORD and wept in anguish. Then she made a vow and said, "O LORD of hosts, if You will indeed look on the affliction of Your maidservant and remember me, and not forget Your maidservant, but will give Your maidservant a male child, then I will give him to the LORD all the days of his life, and no razor shall come upon his head."

And it happened, as she continued praying before the LORD, that Eli watched her mouth. Now Hannah spoke in her heart; only her lips moved, but her voice was not heard. Therefore Eli thought she was drunk. So Eli said to her, "How long will you be drunk? Put your wine away from you!"

But Hannah answered and said, "No, my lord, I am a woman of sorrowful spirit. I have drunk neither wine nor intoxicating drink, but have poured out my soul before the LORD. Do not consider your maidservant a wicked woman, for out of the abundance of my complaint and grief I have spoken until now."

Then Eli answered and said, "Go in peace, and the God of Israel grant your petition which you have asked of Him."

And she said, "Let your maidservant find favor in your sight." So the woman went her way and ate, and her face was no longer sad (1 Sam. 1:2-18).

Had Hannah had her baby yet? No. But the Bible says that she was no longer sad. Hannah hadn't conceived her baby in the natural, but she had conceived her baby in the spirit. She had the word of the Lord, and she knew that this baby was on his way!

What I love about Hannah is she wasn't afraid to get real with God. She had gone up to Shiloh year after year, and finally, this one year, she couldn't take it anymore. She wanted a child, and she was determined to hear from God on the matter. The Scripture says that Hannah was a woman of sorrowful spirit. A lot of us are afraid to say how bad things really are because we think that Christians aren't supposed to feel that way, but Hannah got real with God. She was at the point of grief—the Bible says that she was "in bitterness of soul."

The other wife had tormented Hannah constantly because of her barrenness, and Hannah was overwhelmed with her sorrow. But Hannah didn't stay depressed; she didn't remain bitter and sorrowful. The Scripture says that after she got her word from the priest, which was her word from the Lord, her countenance changed. Her face was no longer sad or sorrowful. She was comforted, and she went out and got something to eat.

Here's the lesson: No matter what burden overwhelms you, no matter what you've been asking God about for year after year, we can do what Hannah did! We can call on the God of the universe—the

One who can take your barrenness away and give you new life, the One who can give you the desires of your heart! Maybe, like Hannah, you are crying out for a baby or, like Ruth, you long for a husband. God remembered them both, and He will remember you. I believe that God is remembering you right now, sister. Receive your promise; receive your answer in Jesus' name! Hannah got her word from God, and she believed it. And her countenance changed.

The Waiting Is Not in Vain

Here's what is so fascinating to me: Hannah wanted a son, but God wanted a prophet for Israel. God had to bring Hannah to the point of desperation so that she was not only crying out to the Lord for a child but was willing to give the child up for the Lord's service. She wanted a son, but God needed a prophet. God had to bring Hannah to the place at which she wanted what God wanted.

Your waiting is not in vain, daughter. God has a purpose in our waiting. Think about it: We're still talking about Hannah's son 3,000 years after he lived! We don't know the names of the other wife's children, do we? But Hannah's determination to press in and get her promise is what makes her a hero. She didn't give up! She was discouraged, yes; she had to cry and scream and come before God, yes! But she didn't give up.

God's set time, His appointed time for you, will not be delayed: "You will arise and have mercy on Zion, for the time to favor her, *yes, the set time, has come*" (Ps. 102:13, emphasis added).

God doesn't promise that things are going to be easy, but He does promise us the victory if we don't give up! We may lose a few battles along the way, but we can easily win the war if God is on our side. If God is for us, who can be against us? God uses the trials and tribulations of life to sharpen us—to strengthen us and to make us more like His Son.

> You [Judah] shall no more be termed Forsaken, nor shall your land be called Desolate any more. But you shall be called

Hephzibah [My delight is in her], and your land be called Beulah [married]; for the Lord delights in you, and your land shall be married [owned and protected by the Lord] (Isa. 62:4, *AMP*).

Prayer

Dear heavenly Father, thank You for Your countless promises in the Bible, and thank You that our waiting, although sometimes long, is never in vain! Lord, I believe that Your set time has come for Your daughters who have been waiting so patiently for Your perfect timing. Lord, You will not tarry but will act on behalf of those who wait for You! And Your daughters shall not be ashamed who wait for You. Lord, give us Your best and nothing less! Help us to hold fast to Your promises, for they shall surely come to pass. Let this be the time and let our joy be full. In Jesus' name, amen.

REFLECTIONS

1. Has God made specific promises to you about your dating and your future marriage life? What are they?
2. What are some Scriptures or Bible stories that God has used to encourage you while you are in your season of waiting?
3. What can we learn from Jensine and Dan's love story?
4. Have you ever made a list of the qualities you're looking for in a husband? Why could this be helpful?

24

TIME TO SHINE!

Then you shall see and become radiant, and your heart shall swell with joy.
ISAIAH 60:5

Those who look to Him are radiant; their faces are never covered with shame.
PSALM 34:5, *NIV*

Let the king be enthralled with your beauty; honor him, for he is your lord.
PSALM 45:11, *NIV*

The journey you've been on, daughter, has likely not been an easy one. If you have been heartbroken, I am certain that your grief has been the hardest thing you've ever been through. Maybe there have been times when you didn't know if you'd make it. But as you have pressed on, your breakthrough has come, or is perhaps very near.

Somehow, by God's grace, you have survived the dark night of the soul. You have passed the test. And you will be rewarded. Now, daughter, it's *time to shine*!

Lazarus, Come Forth!

When Jesus shouted those words, "Lazarus, come forth!" his good friend Lazarus had been in the tomb for four days, his body already starting to decay and the smell of death was all over him. But as the stone in front of the tomb was rolled away, I imagine that the ground shook, and then at Jesus' simple command, Lazarus stumbled out.

The crowd of onlookers standing around the tomb with Jesus most certainly could not believe their eyes. Lazarus was alive! He was breathing. He was no longer among the dead, but by an incredible miracle that many had been eye witnesses to, he had rejoined the living. After the shock wore off, I'm sure there were hugs and tears of joy. Martha and Mary probably ran to their beloved brother whom they had thought they would never lay eyes on again and quickly unwrapped the grave clothes that covered him from head to toe.

Where there had been tears of sorrow and songs of mourning, there were now tears of joy and much laughter. A miracle had taken place. Lazarus, this beloved friend and brother, was now alive!

You will not die, daughter, but you will live and declare the works of the Lord (see Ps. 118:17)! Just as Lazarus did, you will come forth—more radiant, more joyful and more *alive* than ever before!

It's time for you to shine. You have survived those seemingly endless nights in the tomb of sorrow. It's time for you to take those nasty grave clothes off! It's time for you to leave the graveyard and to stop walking among the dead. There's a time to wail over a lost love; there's a time to mourn at his grave; but the truth is, no amount of tears can bring back something that's really dead.

The loss of a significant relationship, whether through divorce, an unexpected breakup or a death, can send us into deep mourning. It's important to grieve, and there is definitely a time to do so. Ecclesiastes 3:4 says that there is "a time to weep, and a time to laugh; a time to mourn, and a time to dance." There's a time to cry until you can't cry anymore when something or someone very important in your life is gone. That kind of loss is great, and by grieving the loss you honor the fact that what you had was important to you. Maybe the person you lost is only across town, or maybe he left you for another person and now lives far away. Whatever the situation, it was like a death. But the good news is, right after this Scripture says that there's a time to weep and mourn, it says that there's "a time to laugh, and a time to dance."

Shaking the Blues

About a year after my breakup with Michael, I decided that it was time to stop mourning. I thought, *Why not throw a Christmas party at my house?* So I began shopping for food and decorations; I even bought a fake Christmas tree and sent out email invitations. I really wanted to celebrate the season.

A few days before my party, I was on my way to Pier One to buy some cute festive glasses to serve eggnog or cider in. Suddenly—I can't really explain how—I felt the Lord's displeasure. As I drove, I thought, *What is going on?* I went to Pier One and looked at the glassware but didn't feel that I was supposed to buy anything. I drove home confused and empty-handed.

Only days earlier, I had been online looking for something fun to do over the holidays and had spotted a Christian singles' cruise. The cold outside in my part of the world made the cruise's ports of call quite tempting, to say the least: the Bahamas, St. Thomas, St. John and St. Martin. I had never been to St. Martin and really wanted to go. The only problem was that the cruise departed out of Ft. Lauderdale on December 15, the same day as my Christmas Party—and I had already sent out invitations.

It was now Wednesday; the ship left on Saturday. As I pondered my confusion over not buying the glassware, I prayed, "Lord, You can't be serious. Do You want me to cancel my Christmas party and go on this Christian singles' cruise?" I felt total peace, unlike how I had felt on my way to Pier One. So with no time to waste, I booked the cruise, reserving my own private cabin, and cancelled my Christmas party.

Everyone was understanding—although I didn't tell people why I had cancelled until I got back from the cruise. The truth was, I hadn't truly wanted to throw a Christmas party! I was simply trying to do something to shake off the blues, and I thought throwing a party was the best way to do it. But anyone who has thrown a party knows that while it is fun, it's also a lot of hard work. God in His infinite mercy, however, didn't let me throw that party. Instead, He had a much grander idea in mind for me.

A Time to Dance

The ship was called the *Oasis of the Seas*. The Royal Caribbean *Oasis* is the largest ocean-going vessel, holding 6,000 guests. It is basically a small floating city having everything a person could possibly want or need while on a vacation, including top-of-the-line shops, restaurants, pools and entertainment of all kinds.

On my first night onboard the *Oasis*, I met the group of about 40 Christian singles that I'd be traveling with—guys and girls from all over the country and several from Canada—in the formal dining room. We had dinner seating at eight thirty every night. Perfect! That way we could take advantage of long days at the pool or excursions at the various ports of call.

I hit it off right away with two guys, Jay and Alex, and also with a girl named Maggie, who was from Texas. I always seem to get along great with Texan women. Most of them are independent, strong and lots of fun!

When we stopped in St. Martin, Maggie and I teamed up on a mountain-biking excursion. Afterward we enjoyed the best fish I have ever eaten as we dined with a perfect view of the water. The weather we enjoyed at that port of call was the best that we had all week—perfectly sunny and tropical.

My favorite part of the cruise, though, was the time we spent on the ship. Jay and Alex were military guys and had the muscles to prove it. They loved working out, and so did I. The ship featured an amazing gym in which we could get our cardio on while we looked out at the deep blue ocean. Jay and Alex were gracious enough to let a girl work out with them, and let me tell you, it was challenging.

I tried to do everything they did. I even did push-ups while doing a handstand against the wall! It was not easy, but it was really fun trying.

I had only been on the cruise for a couple of days when I realized, *I'm not sad. I'm not even thinking about the past.* I was truly enjoying an oasis in the midst of the desert that I had been wandering in for the past year of my life.

Dinner each night was an event. There were two formal nights during the week-long cruise, but I made every night a formal night by dressing the part. If you've ever been on a cruise, you know that the food is one of the main attractions for many, especially during the evening meal in the formal dining room. There's just something about chandeliers and white linen table cloths and coffee served in silver pitchers and four-course meals!

One of my favorite people on the cruise was a young man from Canada named Brian. Brian was only about 25, but his mama must have raised him right, because he was such a gentleman. He knew that I often had a hard time making up my mind about which appetizer to order, because they were all so amazing. I usually picked chilled fruit soup because I'm such a fan of soup, but sometimes I wanted to try the shrimp cocktail or something else. Since I was too embarrassed to order two appetizers, even though there is no limit on the cruise, Brian would say to the waiter in a British-Canadian accent, "Excuse me, waiter, but the laaaadddddyyyy would like a shrimp cocktail." It cracked me up every time. Brian was delightful and a wonderful dinner companion on the cruise.

After dinner it was time to dance! I danced almost every night on the ship—something I hadn't done in a long, long time. I was reminded that the Bible says that there is "a time to dance"! And this was definitely my time.

One night Alex and I danced under the Caribbean stars for hours. It was the last formal night, and several of the guys wore sequined top hats that they had bought in St. Martin. I happened to wear a sequined gold dress that night—the same dress I had worn on my disappointing New Year's Eve dinner with Michael nearly a year ago. Funny thing was, I had almost thrown the dress away, never wanting to think about that night again, but now here I was in that dress, dancing the night away under a Caribbean moon with a handsome and fun guy. That is what I call dress redemption! Give your dress a new memory, and voila! You'll love it again.

Although neither of us were professional dancers, Alex did his best to twirl me around, and we laughed and laughed as the warm tropical breeze made us forget all about the snow and cold back home. It was time to dance! And it was time to shine in my sparkly gold dress.

Alex and I saw each other once after the cruise, but we both agreed that what we had was more of a friendship. I feel certain that God sent Alex and Jay on that cruise just for me. Well, maybe not *just* for me, but the trip sure wouldn't have been the same for me without them.

Time for You to Shine

When I look back on that cruise, the thing I remember most is the dancing! From dancing under the stars with Alex to doing the salsa at the salsa club to dancing with Brian to 80s music, I danced! And I don't think I shed one tear that entire week. After crying a sea of tears all year long, it was a welcome relief to be on the sea laughing and dancing, not crying! This must be the oasis that I needed to find. I didn't realize it would be a cruise ship literally called the *Oasis*. But when we're going through something hard, we need to find an oasis of relief. We need to be kind to ourselves, and we need to enjoy life again. It was time for me to shine!

When we've been hurt, rejected or wounded in a relationship, it's so tempting for us to crawl into our cocoon and hide. We're hurting so bad that we don't want to get out of bed, let alone go on a cruise with a group of 40 people and another 5,960 passengers we've never met before.

But let me tell you, that cruise was worth every penny that it cost me. On it I discovered something profound regarding my situation: I wasn't alone. There is heartache everywhere. In fact, if we tune in, we'll see that it's all around us.

A beautiful lady I met on the cruise had recently been told by her husband of 37 years that he was leaving her for her girlfriend. Wow, I was mourning the loss of a one-year investment, and she was mourning the loss of a nearly four-decade investment that included kids! But in spite of her pain, this woman looked beautiful every night, talked about her love for the Lord and held out hope and forgiveness toward her husband in case he returned and repented. Another man in our group was mourning the loss of a 13-year marriage and was now raising his young daughter on his own.

Everyone had a story. I wasn't alone, and neither are you. Your story is important to God, and when all is said and done, it will have a beautiful and happy ending. But you can't stay in your cocoon. It's time for you to come forth, as Lazarus did from the tomb. Like a butterfly that has emerged from its cocoon, it's time for you to fly again. It's time for you to shine.

> But those who wait upon the LORD shall renew their strength; they shall mount up with wings like eagles, they shall run and not be weary, they shall walk and not faint (Isa. 40:31).

You will not faint, daughter. You are a survivor, and you are stronger than you know. Your story and the pain you have been through have only made you wiser and more compassionate for others who are hurting. Just as with the butterfly working its way out of the cocoon, your struggle to become free has made you stronger. And as you keep your eyes fixed on Jesus, the lover of your soul, your face will become radiant.

You are lovely. You are beautiful. It's time to shine again! Because you, daughter, are a prize to be won!

Prayer

Dear heavenly Father, thank You that our seasons of mourning do end! And thank You that Your word tells us that there is a time to laugh and a time to dance! Father, I pray that every broken heart reading this prayer will feel Your joy—as if someone is literally tickling them!—and they will laugh and dance again. Have mercy on those who are still suffering, and bring them out, Lord! Let them hear Your voice just as Lazarus heard You call, "Come forth!" Lord, we declare and decree that this is our time to come forth out of the grave, to take our grave clothes off and to join the land of the living! We declare over ourselves that it is time to shine again! Make us radiant for Your glory. In Jesus' name, amen.

REFLECTIONS

1. Have you ever felt as if you were like Lazarus coming out of the tomb after a season of mourning?
2. When you have experienced the worst heartache of your life, how have you helped yourself feel alive again? How has God helped you?
3. How does going through heartbreak make us more compassionate toward others and more able to reflect God's glory?

RECIPES

Wendy's Green Smoothie

1 or 2 handfuls of kale (organic if possible)
1 or 2 handfuls of spinach (organic if possible)
A few slices of cucumber with the skin on
Some broccoli (not too much)
1 green apple and/or fresh pineapple
Chia seeds (1 tbsp)
Flaxseed oil or coconut oil (1 tbsp)
A bit of fresh ginger (if you have it)
Celery (if you have it)
Cold water (enough to blend the ingredients)

Combine ingredients and blend in a blender.

Note: I don't use sugar—only fresh fruit to sweeten—and this smoothie is not very sweet. If you like it sweeter, use more fruit or other natural sweeteners such as agave nectar or stevia.

Broccoli-Pineapple Juice

Broccoli
Pineapple or green apple
Ginger

Combine ingredients in a juicer.

Note: Spinach is nice with this too. I love the taste of broccoli and pineapple or green apple together; a bit of ginger or spinach adds even more health benefits plus gives the drink a little zing. You can also add a pinch of turmeric to make it super healthy. Enjoy!

ENDNOTES

Chapter 7: Double-Minded Ways
1. Israel Houghton and Ricardo Sanchez, "Moving Forward" on *The Power of One*, Sony, audio CD, 2009.

Chapter 8: Kansas City, Here I Come!
1. Elisabeth Elliot, *Quest for Love: True Stories of Passion and Purity* (Grand Rapids: Revell, 2002), p. 127.
2. Definition of "palate": www.vocabulary.com/dictionary/palate.

Chapter 10: Guard Your Heart
1. Hebrew definition of "keep thy heart with all diligence": www.hebrew4christians.com/Med itations/Keep_thy_heart/keep_thy_heart.html.
2. Greg Allen, "Keep Your Heart" (sermon, Bethany Bible Church, Portland, OR, September 15, 2002), www.bethanybible.org/archive/2002/091502.htm.

Chapter 11: You Are Worth the Price of Dinner *and* Dessert
1. Darrell Evans, "Your Love Is Extravagant," recorded by Casting Crowns on *Casting Crowns*, Reunion Records, Inc., audio CD, 2003.

Chapter 12: The Red Herring
1. Definition of "red herring": www.en.wikipedia.org/wiki/Red_herring. See also www. tvtropes.org/pmwiki/pmwiki.php/Main/RedHerring.

Chapter 14: The Dangers of Recreational Kissing
1. Elisabeth Elliot, *Passion and Purity* (Grand Rapids: Revell, 2013), p. 127.
2. Ibid., p. 128-29.
3. Ibid., p. 125.
4. Ibid., p. 179.

Chapter 15: Purity Is Sexy
1. Definition of "innocence": www.merriam-webster.com/dictionary/innocence.
2. Definition of "purity": www.dictionary.reference.com/browse/purity.
3. Stacy Hord, *A New Vision for Dating: Finding God's Plan for a New Relationship* (Alachua, FL: Bridge-Logos, 2009).
4. Joshua Harris, *Boy Meets Girl: Say Hello to Courtship* (Sisters, OR: Multnomah, 2005), p. 91.
5. Ibid., p. 152.
6. Ibid., p. 154.
7. Stacy Hord, *A New Vision for Dating*.

Chapter 19: Begin Again
1. Taylor Swift, "Begin Again" on *Red*, Big Machine Records, LLC, audio CD, 2012.

Chapter 22: Be the Prize!
1. Jennifer Grey, "Still Having the Time of My Life 25 Years On: *Dirty Dancing* Star Jennifer Grey on Patrick Swayze, Dancing and Her 'Nose Job from Hell,'" *Mirror*, August 23, 2012. www.mirror.co.uk/3am/celebrity-news/jennifer-grey-on-patrick-swayze-dirty-1274628.

Chapter 23: God's Promises
1. Jensine Bard is the executive producer and host of *Testimony*, a Global Radio broadcast. You can find out more about her at www.jensinebard.com.

Chapter 24: Time to Shine!
1. Francesca Battistelli, "Strangely Dim" on *Hundred More Years Deluxe*, Fervent Records, audio CD, 2013.

**For more about Wendy
and *You Are a Prize to Be Won!***

Website:
www.yourareaprize.com

Twitter:
https://www.twitter.com@wendygcbn

Facebook Author Page:
https://www.facebook.com/wendygriffithcbn